WRITERS AND THEIR WORK

D. H. LAWRENCE

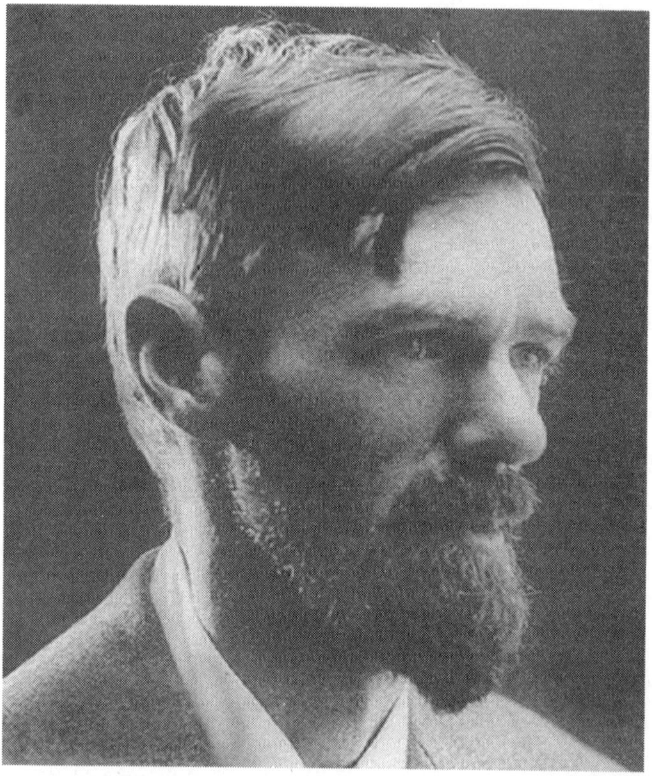

The British Council

D. H. LAWRENCE

D. H. LAWRENCE

Linda Ruth Williams

NORTHCOTE

BRITISH COUNCIL

ATLANTIC
PUBLISHERS & DISTRIBUTORS (P) LTD

This edition is published by
ATLANTIC
PUBLISHERS & DISTRIBUTORS (P) LTD
7/22, Ansari Road, Darya Ganj, New Delhi-110 002
Tel: 40775252, 23273880, 23275880, 23280451; Fax: +91-11-23285873
E-mail: orders@atlanticbooks.com; Web: www.atlanticbooks.com

By arrangement with
Northcote House Publishers Ltd
Horndon House, Horndon, Tavistock, Devon, PL19 9NQ,
United Kingdom. (T)+44(0)1822 810066; (F)+44(0)1822 810034
(E) northcote.house@virgin.net and (W) www.northcotehouse.co.uk
The *Writers and their Work* series is published in association with the British Council.

First Indian Reprint 2010
First published in 1997 by Northcote House Publishers Ltd

ISBN 978-81-269-1283-4

British Library Cataloguing-in-Publication Data
A catalogue record for this book is available from the British Library

Typeset by PDQ Typesetting, Newcastle-under-Lyme
Printed in India at Nice Printing Press, A-33/3A, Site-IV,
Industrial Area, Sahibabad, Ghaziabad, U.P.

For Jake Stedman Williams

Contents

Acknowledgements

I am grateful to participants of the 'D. H. Lawrence and Sexuality' conference held at the D. H. Lawrence Centre, Nottingham University in November 1995 for comments on a draft of chapter 4 which was presented there. Thanks also to Mark Kermode for reading and commenting on the whole draft. Finally, I gratefully acknowledge Laurence Pollinger Ltd and the Estate of Frieda Lawrence Ravagli for granting me permission to quote from Lawrence's works.

Biographical Outline

1885	Born in Eastwood, Nottinghamshire on 11 September, into working-class mining family.
1898–1901	Scholarship to Nottingham High School.
1900–6	Works as pupil-teacher.
1905	Writes his first poems, 'To Campions' and 'To Guelder Roses'.
1906	Begins first novel, *The White Peacock* (then called *Laetitia*) as well as stories and poems, and starts teacher training studies at Nottingham University College.
1907	Short story 'A Prelude' wins *Nottinghamshire Guardian* competition.
1909	Jessie Chambers sends selection of Lawrence's poems to the *English Review*; poems are published in November.
1910	Lawrence's mother dies; Lawrence begins *Sons and Lovers*.
1911	*The White Peacock* published.
1912	*The Trespasser* published. Meets and elopes with Frieda Weekley; travels abroad, to Germany and Italy, for the first time.
1913	*Sons and Lovers* and *Love Poems and Others* published; begins *The Sisters* (which eventually becomes both *The Rainbow* and *Women in Love*).
1914	Frieda divorced; Lawrence and Frieda are married in Kensington. They spend World War I in Berkshire, Sussex and Cornwall. *The Prussian Officer and Other Stories* and the play *The Widowing of Mrs Holroyd* are published.

1915	*The Rainbow* published in September and suppressed in November. Sets up the *Signature* magazine with John Middleton Murry and Katherine Mansfield in the autumn.
1916	Completes version of *Women in Love* in 1916, but because of controversy over *The Rainbow*, fails to find a publisher; *Twilight in Italy* published.
1917	Lawrence is called up and rejected from military service on grounds of ill health. *Look! We Have Come Through!* published.
1918	*New Poems* published.
1919	Lawrence is seriously ill with influenza; Lawrence and Frieda gain passports and live in Italy, Sardinia and Germany 1919–22.
1920	Works on *The Lost Girl, Mr Noon, Aaron's Rod. Women in Love* is finally published in New York 'for subscribers only'.
1921	*The Lost Girl* (published 1920) wins the James Tait Black prize. *Psychoanalysis and the Unconscious, Movements in European History, Sea and Sardinia* all published.
1922	Travels to Ceylon en route to Australia, where he writes *Kangaroo*. Moves on to Taos in New Mexico. *Fantasia of the Unconscious, England My England* and *Aaron's Rod* all published.
1923	Trip to Mexico; begins *The Plumed Serpent*. Return trip to England. *Studies in Classic American Literature, The Ladybird, Kangaroo* and *Birds, Beasts and Flowers* all published.
1924	Frieda given Kiowa Ranch in New Mexico in exchange for manuscript of *Sons and Lovers*; Lawrence writes *The Woman Who Rode Away. The Boy in the Bush* (with Molly Skinner) published.
1925	Lawrence seriously ill with malaria in Mexico; his tuberculosis is diagnosed. The Lawrences return to Europe. *St Mawr, Reflections on the Death of a Porcupine* and *The Princess* all published.
1926–30	Lives in Europe, moving around between Italy, Austria, Germany, Switzerland, Spain and France.

1926 Lawrence visits England for the last time. *The Plumed Serpent* and the stories 'Sun' and 'Glad Ghosts' are all published.

1927 *Mornings in Mexico* published.

1928 Writes 'The Escaped Cock'; *Lady Chatterley's Lover* published privately in Florence. *The Woman Who Rode Away* and *Collected Poems* also published.

1929 Copies of *Lady Chatterley's Lover* and *Pansies* seized in London in January; Lawrence's paintings seized by the police from an exhibition in London in July.

1930 Completes *Apocalypse*. Dies of tuberculosis in March, at Vence in the South of France.

Abbreviations and References

A.	*Apocalypse* (Harmondsworth: Penguin, 1979)
AR	*Aaron's Rod* (Harmondsworth: Penguin, 1977)
CSN	*The Complete Short Novels* (Harmondsworth: Penguin English Library, 1982)
FU	*Fantasia of the Unconscious*, in *Fantasia of the Unconscious and Psychoanalysis and the Unconscious* (Harmondsworth: Penguin, 1974)
L1	*The Letters of D. H. Lawrence*, vol. 1, September 1901–May 1913, ed. James T. Boulton (Cambridge: Cambridge University Press, 1979)
L2	*The Letters of D. H. Lawrence*, vol. 2, June 1913–October 1916, ed. George J. Zytaruk and James T. Boulton (Cambridge: Cambridge University Press, 1981)
L3	*The Letters of D. H. Lawrence*, vol. 7, November 1928–February 1930, ed. Keith Sagar and James T. Boulton (Cambridge: Cambridge University Press, 1993)
LCL	*Lady Chatterley's Lover* (Harmondsworth: Penguin, 1994)
MN	*Mr Noon* (Cambridge: Cambridge University Press, 1984)
P1	*Phoenix: The Posthumous Papers of D. H. Lawrence*, ed. Edward D. McDonald (London: Heinemann, 1936)
P2	*Phoenix II: Uncollected, Unpublished and Other Prose Works by D. H. Lawrence*, ed. Warren Roberts and Harry T. Moore (London: Heinemann, 1968)
Poems	*The Complete Poems of D. H. Lawrence*, ed. Vivian de Sola Pinto and Warren Roberts (Harmondsworth: Penguin, 1977)
PS	*The Plumed Serpent* (Harmondsworth: Penguin, 1977)
R.	*The Rainbow* (Harmondsworth: Penguin, 1979)

SCAL	*Studies in Classic American Literature* (Harmondsworth: Penguin, 1977)
SL	*Sons and Lovers* (Harmondsworth: Penguin, 1994)
T.	*The Trespasser* (Harmondsworth Penguin, 1994)
WL	*Women in Love* (Harmondsworth Penguin, 1989)
WRA	*The Woman Who Rode Away and Other Stories* (Harmondsworth: Penguin, 1978)

Introduction: Life works

Writing about D. H. Lawrence has traditionally been infused with a myth of the individual wrought in epic proportions. With the exception of suicides such as Virginia Woolf or Sylvia Plath, whose deaths have too often been the inscribers of their lives and the critical filter through which their work is read, perhaps no other twentieth-century writer has been so strongly interpreted through the lustre of biography. Lawrence's textual output was large, especially so since he lived only to the age of 44. His life has been glorified as both adventurous and scandalous. His marriage was passionate and stormy, he circled the world, living and writing in a number of exotic locations, he was accused of spying and obscenity, he both abandoned and affirmed the influence of his working-class English roots.

These elements form the components of a compelling life-narrative upon which the history of readings of Lawrence has been pinned. It has, for instance, been almost impossible to read *Sons and Lovers* without some reference to its biographical bedrock: Lawrence's own intense Oedipal relationship with his mother, his development as an artist and estrangement from his class, and his relationship with his adolescent love, Jessie Chambers (Miriam in the novel). Political and sexual attitudes *within the text*, even those emerging from the mouths of characters, have been identified directly as the political and sexual attitudes *of the author*. Critics who might otherwise take the utmost care to avoid directly ascribing nebulous textual meaning to specific authorial source are still happy to write that Lawrence *is* Rupert Birkin (from *Women in Love*), *is* Paul Morel (from *Sons and Lovers*), *is* Aaron Sisson (from *Aaron's Rod*). The two primary movements in critical theory this century which have argued against attributing authorial intention to the text –

I. A. Richards's practical criticism of the 1930s, and the 'death of the author' poststructuralism following, in particular, Roland Barthes's work in the 1960s and 1970s – seem to have had little impact on readings of Lawrence. Here the great man and his meanings have stood full square behind each sentence. This, despite the fact that it was Lawrence who wrote 'Never trust the artist, trust the tale'.

If Lawrence wrote personally, with the power of individual history implicit in every fictional scenario, so Lawrence criticism has often dictated that passionate personal response is the most vigorous way of reading him. The Lawrence we were reading until recently was very much this Lawrence. Jane Davis – an exponent of this mode – sees academic analysis as 'second-hand', charging us to be 'careful that we don't lose the vitality of response [Lawrence] knew was so important to real knowledge': 'It is not enough to be willing to accept Lawrence as an important author', she writes; 'Lawrence demands acceptance as a man, as a thinker, and as an example'.[1] Furthermore, the fact that writers on Lawrence seem to need to tell *their own* stories in writing about Lawrence through *his* stories indicates that something about his work fundamentally problematizes the divisions between writing and self-identity, between the written text and the reader's narrative – for good or ill. F. R. Leavis begins his 1955 eulogy to Lawrence's 'genius' – *D. H. Lawrence: Novelist* – with the admission that he is 'dealing with a writer who has been for me a major contemporary fact'.[2] However, acknowledging his 'own involvement in the history' of Lawrence's development as a writer is in Leavis's case partly bound up with the fact that he was a crucial player in what he calls 'a long battle to win recognition for Lawrence' in the early 1930s.[3] It was largely due to Leavis's (now outmoded) critical efforts that Lawrence achieved his place in the twentieth-century canon. Leavis's aim was unambiguously 'to win clear recognition for the nature of Lawrence's greatness',[4] so in a sense Leavis's story is also the story of Lawrence's critical reception. Since Lawrence's work deliberately blurs the distinction between 'serious' fiction and personalized argument, or between measured presentation and heated involvement, it is tempting to read all of his work as polemic, as opinion-spinning. Shifts in how Lawrence has been read have been dramatic: ever since his death, when Leavis started to write about him seriously in the journal *Scrutiny*, Lawrence's corpus has been a site upon which debates have raged, about how we judge literary worth and, more recently, about what constitutes 'English studies'. It might be said that the history of readings of Lawrence itself constitutes a kind of microcosm of the history of literary criticism this century.

Leavis's personalization is nothing compared to other readings set in the context of a 'what he has meant to me' narrative. A good number of texts written by women begin with an account of how Lawrence, with a close-to-personal touch, seduced them when they reached puberty. Alison Light 'identified desperately' with Miriam in *Sons and Lovers* when she studied the novel for A level,[5] whilst Ursula in *The Rainbow* 'has been' Carol Dix's '*alter ego*, mentor and guide, since teenage years':[6] 'I kept finding myself there on the pages', she writes.[7] In *Lawrence's Men and Women*, Sheila MacLeod recalls

> reading Lawrence at my father's suggestion, indeed insistence, the sort of insistence a benevolent Victorian paterfamilias might have used to induce his daughters to read the Bible: for their own good and betterment. My parents, who spoke as familiarly of Lawrence and Frieda as if they were almost alter egos, were Leavisite enthusiasts.[8]

If Lawrence's life is said to infuse his writings, then writing about him, particularly during the 1950s, 1960s and 1970s, was partly a question of showing that criticism was a 'real', personally felt, and above all 'vital' response activated through one's very life, not just (or primarily) with one's mind. The heady amalgam of life and works turned Lawrence into an Example to us all.

But it is not the example I plan to follow in this book. Indeed, I will enjoy showing just what a deliciously *bad* example Lawrence often was, breaking his own rules and becoming ever more interesting with each act of self-contradiction. However, because of this overbearing bio-critical history, it is with some trepidation that I frame this introduction to Lawrence with his facts of life, since this has been exactly the way in which life-infused readings have come to predominate. Lawrence's literary development, traced chronologically, might have offered a rational framework for this book, but instead I have preferred to work through the dominant issues to which he returns again and again. The way in which we think through the stresses and changes in Lawrence's work has been organized in other critical discussions by chronology (a move from the realism of a mining *mise en scène*, through modernism and Americana, to a return to Nottinghamshire in the Chatterley tales), or through genre (Lawrence as novelist, poet, playwright, philosopher and short-story writer in one career). I want to range across genre and chronology to think about the key issues which continue to dominate his work: sexuality and gender, the construction of identity, subjectivity, power at an individual and institutional level, racial and class differences. These are clearly interdependent, and I hope that to some extent the concerns of these chapters will bleed into each other. This study merges discussion of Lawrence's fiction and non-fiction, taking the different forms of his writing as part of an ongoing project. Each chapter focuses on one aspect of his struggle to rephrase and reconcile key questions which recur across the sweep of his writing career: gender difference as the centre of personal identity and social struggle (in chapter 3); sexual experience – sex acts themselves – as the central Lawrentian event, which involved Lawrence in a protracted battle with censorship law (in chapter 4); and his pervasive challenge to conventional ways of understanding the individual as embedded in home, family and nation (in chapter 2). I start in chapter 1 with an overview of Lawrence's philosophies, and examine some key terms: life, the unconscious, apocalypse, knowledge, writing and the novel.

I will keep returning to the fact that Lawrence must be read as an interdisciplinary thinker who works readily across and between different cultural forms: prose, poetry, fiction (both novels and short stories), drama, painting, travel writing. Although I find myself focusing mostly on the novels in my readings, it is impossible to read Lawrence simply as a novelist – or as a poet, short-story or prose writer. Which is to say both that his view of the novel, or of these other forms, is not simple, and that every element of Lawrence's work is imbued with an overarching philosophical struggle. His work is the site of a singular blurring of literary forms, perhaps an unprecedented refusal of the strictures of genre and knowledge categories. A reading of Lawrence's interdisciplinarity is overdue. I cannot think of another literary figure whose wider cultural agenda and experimentation problematizes the notion of the literary as sovereign form. This is not just because he wrote within four major literary areas, or because his non-fiction crosses into philosophy, biography and psychoanalysis, or even because he painted too, but because each of these activities cross-fertilized, each was undertaken within the context of the other. It would be difficult now to read any of these individual activities as 'pure' forms, and far more interesting to read them as hybrids. In each of these chapters I will weave between writings, and organize my analysis more or less thematically. It is then particularly important to give a strong sense of the broad historical sweep of his work at the outset, so that the readings which follow this have a basic historical anchor.

I offer a brief overview of Lawrence's work, not to draw up a picture of the man behind the work, but to see the corpus as a whole as an ongoing literary-philosophical project with certain dominant elements under constant investigation. Born in 1885 into a working-class family in the Midlands town of Eastwood, son of a miner and a middle-class woman who married below her class, Lawrence grew up in the *fin de siècle* moment of social, sexual and cultural transition, and published his first works as modernism was dawning, in the years preceding the First World War. He had begun writing seriously when he was 19, but it was only when his first girlfriend, Jessie Chambers, sent some of his poems to the *English Review* in 1909, that his literary career got under way; Chambers, he later wrote, was 'like a princess cutting a thread, launching a ship'. So his work began to receive public recognition. He was at this time working as a teacher in Croydon, but after his first novel was published in 1911 he dedicated himself to writing full-time. Lawrence's teaching career had initially been curtailed by a bout of the serious bronchial illness which had blighted his health since at least 1901. He never enjoyed perfect health, and was eventually diagnosed as suffering from tuberculosis, which killed him in 1930.

This first novel was *The White Peacock*, an early copy of which Lawrence managed to place in his mother's hands just before she died in late 1910. It is Lawrence's only substantial work written in the first person. Like his own later novel, *Women in Love*, but rather *more* like George Eliot's much earlier novel *The Mill on the Floss*, *The White Peacock* is the story of the entangled interrelationships of a group of young people in the rural Midlands, noted for a number of things including the strong homoerotic charge which passes between Cyril, the narrator, and George, prefiguring scenes in *Aaron's Rod*, *Women in Love* and 'The Blind Man'. The novel also contains the figure of Annable, who was to reappear in a rather different guise as Mellors in *Lady Chatterley's Lover*. Despite being only his first novel, *The White Peacock* was a kind of literary crisis-point: critic Tony Pinkney sees it as a testing ground for Lawrence's particular brand of English realism, within which his more distinctive later styles and preoccupations are struggling into being – a novel which finds it hard to sustain itself in the form it takes.[9] Lawrence would not write in quite this way again. After four years of revision (he was a tireless and elaborate redrafter of his own work, favouring rewriting tens or even hundreds of pages again from scratch in preference to the minutiae of tinkering), Lawrence was rather weary of *The White Peacock* by the time it appeared – he called it a 'florid prose poem', and wrote that he had 'no faith in myself at the end, and I simply loathe writing'. Yet he can't have been *that* weary, as he was by this point already working on his next novel, *The Trespasser*, and was also beginning *Sons and Lovers*, as well as short stories and poems, which he continued to write alongside longer projects throughout his life. Lawrence was nothing if not prolific: in twenty-five years he was to write many short stories and novellas, and hundreds of poems, in addition to his novels, travel books and non-fictional prose.

In March 1912 he met Frieda Weekley, wife of his German tutor, with whom he quickly eloped to Germany. 'You are the most wonderful woman in all England', he wrote to her, and later, to a friend back in England he eulogized about the romantic and erotic baptism he had undergone with Frieda: 'The world is wonderful and beautiful and good beyond one's wildest imagination. Never, never, never could one conceive what love is, before hand, never. Life *can* be great – quite god-like' (*L*1 414). Frieda had to leave her children behind her with their father, and then faced bitter divorce proceedings, but the

Lawrences were finally married in London in July 1914, and so were in Britain when World War I broke out that year. After revisions probably influenced by Frieda's knowledge of Freudian psychoanalysis, *Sons and Lovers* was published in May 1913. This is the story of Paul Morel, born into a mining family not unlike Lawrence's own, who develops into a budding artist, and struggles to find a sexual connection with women in the shadow of his overwhelming relationship with his mother. His 'tragedy', as Lawrence put it (explicitly likening it to *Oedipus* and *Hamlet*), follows that first plotted out by Paul's brother William, who dies from the struggle. In a famous letter to Edward Garnett from November 1912, Lawrence writes:

> a woman of character and refinement goes into the lower class, and has no satisfaction in her own life. She has had a passion for her husband, so the children are born of passion, and have heaps of vitality. But as her sons grow up she selects them as lovers – first the eldest, then the second. These sons are *urged* into life by their reciprocal love of their mother – urged on and on. But when they come to manhood, they can't love, because their mother is the strongest power in their lives, and holds them. (*L*1 476–7)

One of Lawrence's best-known and best-loved works, *Sons and Lovers* is still basically realist in form, but by the time it came into print Lawrence was already moving on again. A few months before its publication he had started work on a large project, *The Sisters*, his major novelistic venture of the war years – it was eventually split into two books, *The Rainbow* and its sequel *Women in Love*. As he moved from *Sons and Lovers* to *The Sisters*, Lawrence wrote to Edward Garnett, 'I have no longer the joy in creating vivid scenes, that I had in *Sons and Lovers*... I don't care much more about accumulating objects in the powerful light of emotion, and making a scene of them. I have to write differently'. This 'writing differently' develops gradually as Lawrence works through *The Rainbow*, and only fully bears fruit in *Women in Love* itself. *The Rainbow* is the chronicle of a rural family traced across three generations, eventually developing into the story of Ursula Brangwen, often regarded as one of Lawrence's most appealing heroines. *Women in Love* initially focuses on Ursula and her sister Gudrun too, but spins out to involve a wider range of characters in an investigation of new relationships, art, sexuality and modern morbidity. *Women in*

Love traces a move from rooted Englishness to a more nomadic European, unfixed identity, from the Midlands family home of Ursula to the bohemian scene of Gerald's death in central Europe. Although it does not directly address the war, it is explicitly concerned with the moment of its composition. In his Foreword to *Women in Love*, Lawrence wrote 'it is a novel which took its final shape in the midst of the period of war, though it does not concern the war itself. I should wish the time to remain unfixed, so that the bitterness of the war may be taken for granted in the characters'.[10] 'I am going through a transitional stage myself' he wrote in 1914, again to Garnett: 'I feel that this second half of *The Sisters* is very beautiful... It is my transition stage – but I must write to live, and it must produce its flowers, and if they be frail and shadowy, they will be all right if they are true to their hour'(*L*2 134).

Though Lawrence was not fit to be sent to the trenches, the bitterness of the war may also be taken for granted in his and Frieda's experiences during this time. The war years were spent unhappily in England, mostly in Cornwall and Berkshire. In 1917 Lawrence and Frieda were refused passports to leave the country, and felt themselves to be virtual prisoners, under suspicion by the authorities possibly because of Frieda's German background (she was the cousin of Germany's flying ace, the Red Baron). This was the time, however, when they forged strong links with the so-called 'Other Bloomsbury', a group of London intelligentsia including John Middleton Murry, Katherine Mansfield, Dorothy Brett, Lady Ottoline Morrell, Richard Aldington, the poet H.D. (Hilda Doolittle), and the prime minister's daughter-in-law Lady Cynthia Asquith. The Lawrences were finally able to leave in 1919, for Italy, where Lawrence picked up an earlier novel draft, *The Insurrection of Miss Houghton*, the manuscript of which had been left in Germany during the war years. This was finished as *The Lost Girl*, and won the James Tait Black prize in 1921. The year 1920 also saw the publication of *Women in Love* in America – after the suppression of *The Rainbow* in Britain in 1915 on obscenity grounds, Lawrence had been unable to find a publisher for the novel he thought his best, until Thomas Seltzer took it on in New York. He was also at this time working on *Aaron's Rod* (the novel he had begun in 1917), as well as his follow-up to *Sons and*

Lovers, the unfinished *Mr Noon*, which was only eventually published in 1984.

In 1922 the Lawrences set off for Ceylon, beginning a long period of global restlessness. They soon moved on to Australia, where he wrote the novel *Kangaroo*; some sense of Lawrence's experience during the war is reflected in the 'The Nightmare' chapter of this novel. Then the Lawrences decided to move to America, to take up an invitation from Mabel Dodge Luhan to go to live with her in Taos, New Mexico, thus beginning a long association with the town (Frieda was to remain living here after Lawrence's death). Here Lawrence rewrote his literary critical philosophy, *Studies in Classic American Literature* (which he had started in England during the war years alongside *The Rainbow* and *Women in Love*). During a visit to Mexico in 1923, Lawrence began *The Plumed Serpent* (his 'real novel of America' as he wrote to Seltzer), the story of an independent, middle-aged Irish woman, Kate Leslie, who becomes involved with the leaders of a new political-mystical religious movement. It is the consummate statement of Lawrence's so-called 'power period', in which it has been argued he dabbled in authoritarian ideology and developed the particular strain of misogyny for which he became notorious. But Kate's love–hate relationship with the intense resurrected religion of Quetzalcoatl is the frame for her ambivalent relationship with the novel's other three prime characters, Ramón, Cipriano (whom Kate marries), and Ramón's wilfully passive second wife, Teresa, married after the lingering death of his first wife, the vilified Catholic Carlota (perhaps one of Lawrence's most vitriolically misogynistic creations). He also began *The Boy in the Bush*, his 'Western Australia novel' at this time. It was co-written with the Australian writer Mollie Skinner. This collaborative work may have been a more prevalent practice in the modernist groups (we might think here of Ezra Pound's involvement in T. S. Eliot's *The Waste Land*), but it is still important to note that no other canonical British novelist has worked together with another writer to produce an openly co-authored major novel in quite this way, before or since. In late 1923 Lawrence returned to Europe – to Hampstead and then to Paris, Germany, and back to London, before returning to Kiowa Ranch in Taos, then on again to Mexico in 1924. At this time he wrote 'The Woman Who Rode Away', *St Mawr*, and finished *The Plumed Serpent*.

Then, in early 1925 in Mexico City, Lawrence was struck down by more serious illness. Although he was regularly ill with severe doses of 'flu and bronchial problems throughout his life, this time he suffered a dose of malaria which nearly killed him, and here for the first time he was officially diagnosed as having tuberculosis. Lawrence was sneaked back into the USA, concealing his illness from the border authorities who would have refused entry had they known. He was, however, to stay at Kiowa Ranch only for a few months more before leaving America once more, returning to Europe, but moving restlessly between Britain, Germany France, Spain and Italy over the next five years.

Back in Europe, his writing took another turn. If *The Plumed Serpent* had been marked by political-mystical excess and expressive pseudo-religious incantation, peppered with hymns to the great god Quetzalcoatl and eulogies to darkness, the writing which was to dominate this last phase was marked by a kind of post-apocalyptic pastoral, and an explicit eroticism. Lawrence's final literary phase came with the drafting and redrafting of his most sexually outspoken work, the Lady Chatterley story, first as *The First Lady Chatterley* (which he started in 1926), then as *John Thomas and Lady Jane*, and finally as *Lady Chatterley's Lover*: in January 1927 he wrote that 'I am working on an English novel – but so differently from the way I have written before!' and later he was to call it 'a declaration of the phallic reality'. The story of a cross-class affair, in which Lady Chatterley finds sexual fulfilment with her gamekeeper-lover, defying the despondency and post-war malaise which envelope all around her, was only published in Britain in unexpurgated form in 1960 after the celebrated 'trial of Lady Chatterley'. The late 1920s also saw Lawrence energetically continuing his painting, essay writing and poetry (the *Pansies* collection was written in 1928). The paintings were exhibited in London in July 1929, but were quickly seized, also for their ostensible obscenity – they are still not allowed back into Britain. This was the final phase of Lawrence's work, marked by battles with the morality police, struggles to get into print, but also some welcome financial security as his earlier books began to sell and his reputation developed. From mid-1927, however, his illness grew more serious, and Lawrence tried a number of different, but ultimately unsuccessful, cures. He died in Vence, in France, on 2 March 1930. His ashes are now at Kiowa Ranch in Taos, where Frieda is also buried.

The story of Lawrence's writings and what they have meant to different cultures at different moments continues to be redrafted. Indeed, we might want to map literary history onto this life-history, for Lawrence's life is matched squarely with the term of modernism. He was born in 1885, firmly within the decade which also saw the births of Virginia Woolf, Ezra Pound, T. S. Eliot, James Joyce and Katherine Mansfield. He died as the movement's energies were mutating into the rather different literary forms of the thirties. Although I have said that – roughly speaking – Lawrence's earlier works are marked by the formal qualities of Georgian realism, and as his work during the war progresses he moves away from this and develops other ways of working, his relationship with 'classic modernism' is problematic. Indeed, his writing has only recently been read for its modernist elements, and against the grain of his own vehement critique of his experimental contemporaries. Nevertheless, Lawrence's writing career – from 1909 to 1930 – spans the broad sweep of high modernism, and 'modernism' is a term which will recur throughout this study.

Yet a modernist interpretation of the myth of Lawrence's life events as well as his stories might also be possible: the wandering, classless intellectual, whose artistic identity was fractured across a number of forms, but who was nevertheless desperate to construct a discourse of wholeness to 'shore against [his] ruins'. This tension, between discontinuity and totality, between breakdown and unity, between exile and return, is central to the drama of his fictions. The crucial role Lawrence's writings play in our understanding not just of early twentieth-century literature, but of the development of British cultural and sexual identity throughout this century, is what this book aims to highlight. The paradoxes which fissure his work – as both sexual liberator *and* high puritan, as saboteur *and* saviour of the unified literary ego, as Englishman oscillating between home and homelessness – will underpin this study of the divided Lawrence.

1

Philosophies: The quick, the dead, and 'the old stable ego'

Looking across Lawrence's literary career, a number of persistent questions arise. He wrote during the period of 'high modernism', but is he a modernist? He wrote novels, poems, plays, but also essays, letters, literary criticism, philosophy, psychology, history; he painted too. So, is his work primarily or most significantly literary? He began life as Britain's most famous working-class writer, married an aristocrat, moved restlessly from country to country as a loose member of the international intelligentsia, and declared that 'one can belong absolutely to no class' ('Autobiographical Sketch', *P2*, 595), so how would we fix him socially? He circled the world writing of, and from, and about, every place he lived in, yet whilst he (mostly) wrote in English, his fiction is not solely the chronicle of an Englishman abroad, or an Englishman writing of home from abroad. In particular, he wrote extensively of and in Mexico and the USA, and America published him when Britain wouldn't. His work can be read as an extensive critique of Englishness, although this might be the one thing which *does* mark him as English. How then would we judge the national identity of his writing?

The work of this chapter is to answer some of these questions by exploring Lawrence's key positive terms: sex, life (or 'quickness'), darkness, unconsciousness or blood-consciousness. These are not terms which stand alone, for the structures of Lawrence's thought are oppositional – he is a metaphysician, a dialectician, his terms of preference or celebration are always placed in a relationship of conflict or opposition with terms of condemnation. The page is then something of a philosophical battleground. Against active and healthy sexuality, he poses as negative terms consciousness and cerebral states of being, knowledge or sex 'in the head'. Life is not opposed to death proper, but to a kind of living death which is the result, for Lawrence, of degenerate modern existence. 'We have to choose between the quick and the dead', he writes in his 1925 essay 'The Novel': 'The quick is God-flame, in everything.... the sum and source of all quickness, we will call God. And the sum and total of all deadness we may call human' (*P2* 419–20) Underpinning this is a bitter and very grounded critique of industrialized, over-cerebral humanity as well as, at its opposite, a celebration of life forms and artistic expressions which have freed themselves of 'deadness'.

SELF AND SEX

> The wild creatures are coming forth from the darkest Africa inside us ('The Novel and the Feelings', *P1* 756)

Each of my opening questions suggests transition and instability – the classic issues of modernism, an artistic movement centrally concerned with flux, dissonance, difficulty, and the refusal of the ostensibly accessible, dependable values and structures of Victorian or Edwardian culture. In 1914, as Lawrence was moving away from the experimental realism of *Sons and Lovers* and embarking on new writing in *The Sisters*, he wrote to Edward Garnett that he wanted to challenge 'the old stable ego of the character':

> There is another ego, according to whose action the individual is unrecognisable... [D]on't look for the development of the novel to follow the lines of certain characters: the characters fall into the form of some other rhythmic form, like when one draws a fiddle-bow across a fine tray delicately sanded, the sand takes lines unknown. (*L2* 183)

Thus he began to pen new forms of literary subjectivity which would not only be true to their moment, but which would risk and challenge conventions of the novelistic self. Neither controlled nor unified, nor primarily rational, Lawrentian subjectivity figured in characters or figured-out in essays is messy, sometimes perverse, always divided. In the late poem 'Death is not Evil, Evil is Mechanical', the self is

a thing of kisses and strife
a lit-up shaft of rain
a calling column of blood
a rose tree bronzey with thorns
a mixture of yea and nay
a rainbow of love and hate
a wind that blows back and forth
a creature of beautiful peace, like a river
and a creature of conflict, like a cataract

(*Poems*, 714)

The self he was to struggle to represent in his post-*Sons and Lovers* work does not know what it is at all times, is not even *the same thing* at all times, and seldom acts with the assurance of rational and conscious control. Lilly in *Aaron's Rod* calls himself 'a vagrant...or a migrant', transformed by physical change: 'Do you think a cuckoo in Africa and a cuckoo in Essex is one and the same bird?' (*AR* 337). Lawrence's writing offers an alternative map of the subject. Its modernism lies not in formal experimentation but in the way that it articulates human indefiniteness in a world without the god of organized religion. In the colonial metaphor of my epigram (which makes Africa an image of the unconscious), we each have a 'dark continent', alienated by education but finally undermining our glib sense of self-control.

Spontaneity not predictability, contrariness not conformity, unknowing not certainty, these are the prime virtues the Lawrentian subject can display. And whilst he might finally champion unity over contradiction, it is the divided self which he spends most time picking over. One strain which links Lawrence's work to that other crucial development which grew alongside literary and artistic modernism – Freudian psychoanalysis – is an emphasis on the predominant power of the unconscious, on the unconscious as the controlling element within the self which pervasively challenges the rational subject's self-control. Perhaps surprisingly, in his two famous polemics against classic Freudian psychoanalysis, *Fantasia of the Unconscious* and *Psychoanalysis and the Unconscious*, Lawrence tried to refute psychoanalysis's emphasis on (as he saw it) a sexual motivation underpinning all conscious action ('Only don't let us have sex for tea. We've all got too much of it under the table, and really, for my part, I prefer to keep mine there, no matter what the Freudians say about me', (*FU* 20)). I think that he gets Freud wrong, reading psychoanalysis as an anti-sexual discourse which nevertheless persists in seeing sex everywhere, crudely mapping the wilfully sex-obsessed subject 'as nothing but a monster of perversity, a bunch of engendering adders, horribly clotted' ('The Novel and the Feelings', *P*1 759). Perhaps this is actually truer of Lawrence's fictions than Freud's. Lawrence's stories tell of selves struggling with their own divided desires and unknown motivations, and, as he says later in *Fantasia* (rather contradicting himself), of 'Sex [as] our deepest form of consciousness... utterly non-ideal, non-mental' (*FU* 173).

The term 'antihumanism' gained currency in the 1980s as the poststucturalist critique of the integrated or unified human subject took hold. Antihumanism opposes the traditional humanist notion of the individual as occupying a sovereign space at the centre of the universe of knowledge, power and language. It is, then, literally anti-humanist, anti the post-Renaissance humanist view of the self or subject as one who is ultimately in rational control of herself and her world. Humanism places the human being at the centre of the known world. Antihumanism offers a *de*centred view of the human subject, arguing that the subject is manipulated by desires and forces she may not even be consciously aware of. A Freudian antihumanism would thus argue that the self can never be entirely rational and self-controlled, but is moved rather by unconscious desires and motivations. The unconscious is thus for Freud the decentring principle which acts on the subject, controlling it rather than being controlled by it.

Lawrence's philosophy, based on a principle of unconscious 'life' as the fundamental force which moves and determines our actions, is similarly antihumanist. His growing suspicion of 'the old stable ego' is part of a move to cast new forms for the subject. Lawrence's unconscious is not the absence of awareness, or the Freudian mental state, but is sometimes termed 'blood consciousness', an alternative understanding. It has sex at its heart. Representations of sex are also perhaps the most notorious element in Lawrence's work, bringing him into conflict with censors and moral prescribers throughout his life and after. But 'sex' – by which Lawrence means something beyond straightforward sexual acts, encompassing all thought and behaviour charged with unconscious passion – must also be read as the disruptive spirit which destabilizes older notions of the mentally governed human subject, connecting Lawrence's work to wider concerns in modernist culture. Sex thus challenges the sense that we are in conscious control of our individual domain, undermining the 'ideal' conscious self. Sex is the self's irrationalizing force. It is then sex which underpins the self's contrariness, which ensures her unknowing, which divides self from self within the self. Towards the end of *Fantasia*, Lawrence offers guarded applause to Einstein's Theory of Relativity for knocking 'the last centre-pin out of our ideally-spinning universe' (although in *St Mawr* he also laments a modernism which deems that 'There is nothing to believe in, so let us undermine everything', (*CSN* 341)). Sex similarly decentres the ideally centred self, unravelling the 'old stable ego ... of the character'. Lawrence's selves are less than integrated, more self-undermining, dissatisfied, contradictory. Rejection of the consummate subject is central to a more generalized dissatisfaction, a restlessness which pervades his work.

I will say much more about sex throughout this book, but particularly in chapter 4, where what actually happens in Lawrentian intercourse will be scrutinized alongside further discussion of sex *as* Lawrence's unconscious. For now, let us think briefly about a curious passage at the end of the essay which opens *Studies in Classic American Literature*, called 'The Spirit of Place'. Here Lawrence introduces something he calls the 'IT'. Since *Studies* is a set of literary criticisms (of Poe, Whitman, Melville etc.), what Lawrence is initially trying to do here is find the IT beneath the conscious purpose of literature and use this IT to deconstruct the surface meanings of the text, discerning that which the text is saying but which it doesn't *mean* to say or *know* that it's saying. The IT, in other words, is the repressed of American literature, which animates it 'from beneath'. *Studies*, with its heavy reliance on this IT, was first published in 1923, the same year that Freud introduced the term 'Das Es' in the publication of *Das Ich und Das Es* (*The Ego and the Id*). In this text Freud himself traces the term back to George Groddeck's 'It' (from *The Book of the It*). Paraphrasing Groddeck's notion that 'we are "lived" by unknown and uncontrollable forces', Freud adds that IT or Es might be terms 'for whatever in our nature is impersonal and, so to speak, subject to natural law'.[1] When 'our nature' has to subject itself to 'natural law', the IT presides from beneath. Lawrence's IT, or Freud's Id, is thus the corporeal force which forces us to be suspicious of our notions of personal freedom and control. In this spirit Lawrence writes,

> We are not the marvellous choosers and deciders we think we are. IT chooses for us, and decides for us ... We are free only so long as we obey. (*SCAL* 13)

And just as Freud writes that we are 'lived', so for Lawrence a text is 'written' by an alien force:

> But what we *think* we do is not very important. We never really know what we are doing... We are only the actors, we are never wholly the authors of our own deeds or works.' IT is the author, the unknown inside or outside us. (*SCAL* 26)

Lawrence's purpose in all this is to demonstrate the subversive impact of the IT, which has the ability to betray and show up the author as a rather scheming, egotistical being. The work of art begins to take on an identity of its own; it struggles to have its say, to mean perhaps many different things, against the author's equal desire to control the life of the work of art once it has left his control:

> Two blankly opposing morals, the artist's and the tale's. Never trust the artist. Trust the tale. The proper function of a critic is to save the tale from the artist who created it. (*SCAL* 8)

Texts are then almost as 'alive' as people are, and what is true of literature for Lawrence is also true of selves. The IT is the self's unconscious driving force. IT is 'the dusky body' (*SCAL* 14) which contradicts the 'vulgarly cocksure' 'upper' self (as he characterizes conscious or mental identity in *Fantasia*), which unseats higher idealistic purposes (like democracy, moral action, bodiless spirituality), which *acts*, and makes the self act, unbeknownst to her. If we are not in conscious control as 'we *think* we are' (some other 'I' controls instead – a non-thinking one), then all sense of personal freedom goes out of the window. The IT 'acts' and 'lives' us; we are its puppets, but it is also us. This we may 'know' nothing about:

> Men are not free when they are doing just what they like. The moment you can do just what you like, there is nothing you care about doing. Men are only free when they are doing what the deepest self likes.... If one wants to be free, one has to give up the illusion of doing what one likes, and seek what IT wishes done. (*SCAL* 13)

But to think of Lawrence's selves as divided between IT and I is almost to think of the IT as an alien, inhabiting, parasitic being. Individual 'liberty' is dependent upon 'discover[ing] IT, and...fulfil[ling] IT' (*SCAL* 13),

> IT being the deepest *whole* self of man, the self in its wholeness, not idealistic halfness. (*SCAL* 13)

In a sense Lawrence's project concerns reaching some kind of recognition and incorporation of that IT. Elsewhere IT has other names – darkness, quickness, blood-consciousness. In the essay on Benjamin Franklin, he calls 'The soul of man...a dark vast forest, with wild life in it' (*SCAL* 17), continuing later, 'This is what I believe':

> *'That my known self will never be more than a little clearing in the forest. That gods, strange gods, come forth from the forest into the clearing of my known self, and then go back.'* (*SCAL* 22)

The forest reappears in 'The Novel and the Feelings', in that curiously dubious image with which I began this section. '[T]he forest is inside all of us', he writes, 'and in every forest there's a whole assortment of big game and dangerous creatures, it's one against a thousand' (*P*1 756). To my knowledge, it is only in *Studies* that Lawrence explores this IT so specifically as the self's governing underbelly, exposing its basic structural division, although he returns to the basic issue of division and the control of the internal other across his work – in 'The Novel and the Feelings' the 'dark continent' is 'the *cause* of us and of our days'. I want to flesh this discussion out by defining a much more specific – perhaps a more conscious – force: 'life', or 'quickness'.

'VIVID LIFE'

The IT is the governing undercurrent of the self, but Lawrence's selves do not always swim with IT. 'IT drives us and decides us' he writes, only 'if we are living people, in touch with the source' (*SCAL* 13). So what is the source? Lawrence's literary subjects are frequently the vehicles which bear forth and represent the rather nebulous but crucial key term, 'life'. 'It is life which is the mystery', says Birkin in *Women in Love*: 'Death is hardly mysterious by comparison'. Lawrentian 'life' (or quickness) means many things, and definitions of it can seem contradictory. If 'sex' is not just sexual acts, then 'life' does not mean bare biographical co-ordinates, the personal or familial elements of a life fixed in history or geography. Nor is it simply the intangible quality which animates organic matter. 'Life' is Lawrence's governing philosophical principle, a celebrated term which recurs again and again across the varying range of his works, is present within the natural organic and inorganic world, and we lose touch with it at our peril. In the 1928 essay 'New Mexico' he advocates religious practice within which

> the whole life-effort of man was to get his life into direct contact with the elemental life of the cosmos, mountain-life, cloud-life, thunder-life, air-life, earth-life, sun-life. To come into immediately *felt* contact, and so derive energy, power, and a dark sort of joy. (*P*1 146–7)

Perhaps, then, it is a more precarious as well as a more all-pervasive quality than Freud's unconscious. Vulnerable to industrial destruction, it is profoundly affected by history. Increasingly ignored by the post-World War I 'lost generation' – the over-cerebral bluestocking females and weak-willed males whose mode of being Lawrence laments in 'Women are so Cocksure' and 'On Being a Man' – it is the fundamental governing principle of his ideal subjectivity, and the source of sexual salvation in his last novel. It cuts across differences between the organic and the inorganic. It casts Lawrence as a neo-Romantic, or a pantheist: in 'New Mexico' he calls his a natural not supernatural religion, and he specifically explores pantheism in 'Pan in America' and in *St Mawr*, where Pan is 'the god that is hidden in everything' (*CSN* 326), living particularly vibrantly in the horse of the story's title. And Lawrence's own apparent enthusiasm for living his own life has infused the eulogies of Lawrentians ever since: 'One can only *live* one's soul', he writes in 'Hymns in a Man's Life'; 'The business is to live, really alive' (*P*2 599). Even Lawrence's on-and-off friend

Richard Aldington pays homage by avoiding, in his Introduction to the 1932 edition of *Apocalypse*, 'that quasi-professorial solemnity of the intellectuals which annoyed Lawrence and which is so unsuitable when writing about a free spirit who loved life' (*A*. v). This sentiment was in turn dutifully echoed in the anonymously penned biographical legend at the start of every Penguin edition of his work: 'Lawrence spent most of his short life living'.

This principle is fundamental to every aspect of Lawrence's work, painting as well as writing. In the important essay 'Reflections on the Death of a Porcupine', written at Kiowa Ranch in 1925, he develops a bizarre sub-Darwinian theory of evolution, in which an organism is positioned on the evolutionary scale as an effect of how 'vividly alive' it is: 'Life is more vivid in the dandelion than in the green fern, or than in a palm tree' he writes. But he also judges intensity of life in terms of the ability to survive (through consuming 'lesser' beings; Lawrence never had much sympathy for vegetarians), and to 'do more than survive', to 'really *vive*, live'. Beyond *sur*vival – the basic economy and survival of existence – there is then '*vival*', or vitality, a rather more mystical, and individualistic, category. Lawrentian vitality comes directly from 'the Holy Ghost'. 'In the seed of the dandelion' he continues, 'sits the Holy Ghost in tiny compass':

> the ultimate source of all vitality is in that other dimension, or region, where the dandelion blooms, and which men have called heaven (*P*2 469)

> The Holy Ghost is that which holds the light and the dark, the day and the night, the wet and the sunny, united in one little clue.... Vitality depends upon the clue of the Holy Ghost inside a creature, a man, a nation, a race. When the clue goes, the vitality goes. (*P*2 470–71)

The cockerel in the curious post-Christian tale 'The Escaped Cock' becomes a sign, for the risen Christ (who is resurrected back into fleshly life not heavenly after-life), of a vitality he has yet to grasp and embody, fresh as he is from the tomb. Despite the fact that the bird is, like the social human for Lawrence, 'strangled by a cord of circumstance' (his foot is tied by a piece of string, so he cannot fly off), 'life' finds specific expression in his form. He exudes an intense vividness; he is the apex, the 'crest' of a 'short, sharp wave of life'. Lawrence saw the ego as prime impediment to expressed liveliness. If the cock can defy his tether, we should be able to break the bounds of egoistic consciousness which forms the barrier between us and full reverie in 'life'. The poem 'Ego-Bound' from the *Pansies* collection, explores this: the ego-bound man is

> pot-bound
> in the pot of his own conceit,
> and he can only slowly die.
>
> Unless he is a sturdy plant.
> Then he can burst the pot,
> shell off his ego
> and get his roots in earth again,
> raw earth
>
> (*Poems*, 474–5)

The cock gives the man the clue of how to do this. '[T]he flame of life burned up to a sharp point in the cock. (*CSN* 569), and soon it bursts up into a point in the man, because in bursting out of the old self Christ learns about sex. In Lawrence's wider developing philosophy, the true expression of the cockerel's zestiness is Phallic masculinity, a principle which Lawrence comes to emphasize more and more as his work continues. The ego-bound man bursts the pot, the cock breaks his tether, and the old Christ becomes a new man when a woman begins to arouse him:

> Then slowly, slowly, in the perfect darkness of his inner man, he felt the stir of something coming: a dawn, a new sun. A new sun was coming up in him, in the perfect inner darkness of himself. He waited for it breathless, quivering with fearful hope...'Now I am not myself – I am something new...'... ... He crouched to her, and he felt the blaze of his manhood and his power rise up in his loins, magnificent....'I am risen!' (*CSN* 595–6)

Risen indeed. Life, then – vivacity, zest, vitality – is a sexual response. Or to put it another way, one cannot live without sex – but this is sex in its widest possible sense, sex as a way of plugging into the 'oceanic'. 'The Escaped Cock' re-articulates Birkin's scorn of death in the face of life:

> And the man who had died watched the unsteady, rocking vibration of the bent bird, and it was not the bird he saw, but one wave-tip of life overlapping for a minute another, in the tide of the swaying ocean of life. And the destiny of life seemed more fierce and compulsive to him even than the destiny of death. The doom of death was a shadow compared to the raging destiny of life, the determined surge of life. (*CSN* 563)

This is the Lawrence who has divided readers – the prophet of an alternative mystical sexuality who speaks in the voice of humourless pseudo-mystical didacticism. Curiously un-English, this voice asserts poetic 'truths' which the reader can only accept or reject – it is discomforting, and offers no obvious middle way or compromise response. If there is a 'message' in these writings, it is to choose life, verve, quickness. At its very simplest, we know that Paul Morel will survive when, in the last sentence of *Sons and Lovers*, he walks 'towards the faintly humming, glowing town, *quickly*'. The novel's last word is not a measure of speed, but of vitality.

THE UNCLEAN WORLD

Against this celebrated 'quickness' must be set its opposite. 'The real principle of Evil is not anti-Christ or anti-Jehovah, but anti-life', wrote Lawrence to his sister-in-law in 1929 (*L7* 331–2). The betrayal of 'life' is at the root of Lawrence's ongoing critique of Western consumerism and industrial development. In particular, contemporary England and Englishness is targeted: however far he travelled from England, Lawrence continued to write his way through a nagging anxiety about (as he saw it) its industrial destruction, and this underpins national and racial discussions which developed as he travelled across the world, exploring non-Northern European sensibilities in Italy, southern France, and in the ex-colonies – Ceylon, Australia, the USA. Looking through the windows of someone else's culture only made him think harder about his own. 'I am an Englishman, and I do my bit for the liberty of England', he wrote not from England but from Italy (*L7* 369): 'my Englishness is my very vision'. Lawrence's world-scale critique is perhaps the simple extrapolation of a more specific and ongoing anxiety about the decay of his birthplace, about the condition of early twentieth century Britain, and about Englishness. 'The Island of Great Britain had a wonderful terrestrial magnetism or polarity of its own, which made the British people', he writes in 'The Spirit of Place' in *Studies*. In *St Mawr* a group of riders, out on an expedition, come upon 'one of those places where the spirit of aboriginal England still lingers, the old savage England, whose last blood flows still in a few Englishmen, Welshmen, Cornishmen' (*CSN* 335). But this has been damaged, perhaps irreparably, scarred by industrialism ('the English air: it was never quite free of the smell of smoke, coal-smoke', (*CSN* 372)), war ('Even on this countryside the dead hand of the war lay like a corpse decomposing', (*CSN* 331)), and a nebulous 'evil' which in a moment of dystopian vision, the story's heroine Lou Witt sees sweeping the known world: 'There was no relief. The whole world was enveloped in one great flood. All the nations, the white, the brown, the black, the yellow, all were immersed in the strange tide of evil that was subtly, irresistibly rising' (*CSN* 340). This is focused on the wild body of the stallion of the title, whose essentially phallic spirit is jeopardized by the English folk who want him shot. Determining to take the horse away from 'the tepid and the lukewarm' place where it never even gets properly dark ('the darkness... shook with the concussion of many invisible lights, lights of towns, villages, mines, factories, furnaces', (*CSN* 372–3)), Lou and her mother, both American, finally see England's problems as rooted in the emasculation of 'life':

> The two American women stood high at the window, overlooking the wet, close, hedged-and-fenced English landscape. Everything enclosed, enclosed, to stifling. The very apples on the trees looked so shut in, it was impossible to imagine any speck of 'Knowledge' lurking inside them. Good to eat, good to cook, good even for show. But the wild sap of untameable and inexhaustible knowledge – no! Bred out of them. Geldings, even the apples. (*CSN* 361)

Gender is intrinsic even to the most ostensibly non-gendered of situations in Lawrence. Sex-as-life is fundamental to everything. At this stage in Lawrence's writing at least – before the sexualized return home which comes with *Lady Chatterley* – England has died in losing its sex. Thus Lawrence asks in 'The Spirit of Place',

> For the moment, [England's] polarity seems to be breaking. Can England die? And what if England dies? (*SCAL* 12)

England's death is then part of, and a particularly keen example of, a world-scale 'death' Lawrence keeps working over, nagging at. It takes many forms. Sometimes, like a creeping body-horror, it is a well dressed, Western, civilized spectacle – perhaps the spectacle of civilization itself ('Never draw blood', he writes in *St Mawr*. 'Keep the haemorrhage internal, invisible', (*CSN* 342)). Often – and this is what has linked Lawrence to a particularly individualistic form of fascism – the diatribe is nothing more than a ranting horror at mass civilization, democracy, humanitarianism. A letter written to Lady Cynthia Asquith in 1915 echoes E. M. Forster's conclusion to *Howards End*, which laments the 'red rust' of industrial housing creeping ever nearer to the feudal domain of Howards End itself. Writing from Littlehampton on the Sussex coast, Lawrence sees in the sea and the untouched shore signs that life is still present at the edges of degenerate development: 'It is a great thing to realize that the original world is still there – perfectly clean and pure, many white advancing foams, and only the gulls swinging between the sky and the shore' (*L2* 375). If life, rather than consciousness or rationality or even emotion, ought to be the governing principle of individuality, but modern humanity has worked only to contradict this, then 'life' will be most present where people are not. The 1915 letter goes on,

> It is this mass of unclean world that we have superimposed on the clean world that we cannot bear. When I looked back, out of the clearness of the open evening, at this Littlehampton dark and amorphous like a bad eruption on the edge of the land, I was so sick I felt I could not come back: all these little amorphous houses like an eruption, a disease on the clean earth (*L2* 375)

This is so much like the feeling which comes over Ursula and Skrebensky in *The Rainbow*, when they are staying at Arundel (near to where Lawrence penned this letter). Looking out over the Sussex weald as dawn breaks, Skrebensky can only think of the awakening human race with dismay: 'He too realized what England would be in a few hours' time – a blind, sordid, strenuous activity, all for nothing, fuming with dirty smoke and running trains and groping in the bowels of the earth, all for nothing' (*R.* 466). An opposition of cleanness, health, nature and life is set against dirt, disease, civilized and industrial control, with the first set of terms always privileged.

Thus it follows that the 'bad eruption' of industrialized humanity must be challenged if the clean world is to survive: 'The world is lovely if one avoids man', he wrote to Aldous Huxley in 1929 (*L7* 276), and in the posthumously published poem 'People' (from *More Pansies*), he rephrases this as a need for space:

> I like people quite well
> at a little distance.
> I like to see them passing and passing
> and going their own way,
> especially if I see their aloneness alive in them.
>
> Yet I don't want them to come near.
> If they will only leave me alone
> I can still have the illusion that there is room enough
> in the world.
>
> (*Poems*, 602)

For all the subtlety and complex understandings of his novelistic characterizations, a ruthlessness pervades Lawrence's non-fictional attempts at social clarification. In 1929 he wrote of the Mediterranean, 'When the morning comes, and the sea runs silvery and the distant islands are delicate and clear, then I feel again, only man is vile'. The two poles – the purity of the sea, and the ghastliness of the contemporary English – are pitched against each other: 'I feel much better in the strong light of this sea. But still the thought of the Great British Public puts me off work entirely'. Indeed, at times misanthropy becomes murderous, as he is occasionally even willing to see human beings wiped out altogether – an apocalyptic urge, which Frank Kermode explored in his important study of 1973. It is then perhaps not surprising that Lawrence was suspected of spying during the war, considering his occasional appreciation of Germany's ability to 'burst the bound hide of the cabbage' ('Where do I meet a man or a woman who does not draw deep and thorough satisfaction from this war?' he continues, (*P1* 407)). Although Lawrence is best known for his pacifism at this time (and *this* was actually seen as more treasonable than anything else), in commending Germany for daring to grasp the nettle of violence (Paul Delaney writes that he 'sympathised with the *style* of Germany's actions')[2] he is in part referring here to what Freud was to call the death drive: the governing psychic force which in part explains the existence of sadism, and pleasure in the act and spectacle of destruction, which Freud crystallized in the 1920 publication of *Beyond the Pleasure Principle*. Lawrence also liked the idea of the cultural and national psychic slate being wiped clean, relishing the possibility that the 'disease' of modern Englishness might be 'cured' through extinction. Apocalypse has its attractions. 'The only permanent thing is *consummation* in love or hate', the letter to Asquith concludes.

The *Studies* essay on Edgar Allan Poe, written in 1924, focuses this argument in individual terms. Here Poe is cast as a writer of decay, wreaking a necessary apocalypse on the (here diseased *American*) psyche,

> because old things need to die and disintegrate, because the old white psyche has to be gradually broken down before anything else can come to pass. (*SCAL* 70)

All of these statements, hostile and antisocial, must also be read as part of Lawrence's continuing effort to break with that 'old stable ego'. A certain conception of commercial-cerebral man as 'vile' remains the object of Lawrence's sporadic vilification, part of an ongoing dissection of 'the old white psyche'. Elsewhere in *Studies*, Walt Whitman is praised as the poet 'of the end of life', a great 'post-mortem poet',

> of the transitions of the soul as it loses its integrity. The poet of the soul's last shout and shriek, on the confines of death *Après moi le déluge*.
>
> But we have all got to die, and disintegrate.
> We have got to die in life, too, and disintegrate while we live.
> But even then the goal is not death.
> Something else will come.
>
> (*SCAL* 179)

Death, then, is primarily for Lawrence a kind of 'born again' experience which the vivid soul will undergo in order to come into quickness. Christ in 'The Escaped Cock' must die before he can 'rise', in resurrection or erection. Writers of disintegration are thus crucial interpreters of the apocalypse, articulating the ways in which the slate will be wiped clean. In the late poem 'The Breath of Life', destruction is cast as a life-force:

> The breath of life is in the sharp winds of change
> mingled with the breath of destruction
>
> (*Poems*, 698)

What is to come is something else, the 'new heaven and new earth', perhaps, which Ursula sees at the end of *The Rainbow*:

> And the rainbow stood on the earth. She knew that the sordid people who crept hard-scaled and separate on the face of the world's corruption were living still, that the rainbow was arched in their blood and would quiver to life in their spirit, that they would cast off their horny covering of disintegration, that new, clean, naked bodies would issue to a new germination, to a new growth, rising to the light and the wind and the clean rain of heaven. She saw in the rainbow the earth's new architecture, the old, brittle corruption of houses and factories swept away, the world built up in a living fabric of Truth, fitting to the over-arching heaven. (*R.* 496)

Vehemently anti-industrial, this is also one of Lawrence's clearest articulations of the link between critique and positive assertion. 'Casting off' and 'sweeping away' is followed by new growth, rising life and natural building. The novel thus concludes on a note which manages to be both misanthropic and idealistic at the same time. Water (here rain) is still the element of apocalypse: in the words of 'Death is not Evil', this is Lawrence not as the river 'of beautiful peace' but the 'creature of conflict . . . a cataract'. If, in Lou Witt's pessimism in *St Mawr*, the world-scale 'evil will against any positive living thing' (*CSN* 342) touches her in the form of 'dark-grey waves of evil rearing in a great tide' (*CSN* 340), elsewhere Lawrence posits another flood – a 'good' flood if you like – to wipe away the effects of the bad: the sea in the misanthropic rants of the letters, Whitman's deluge, Ursula's rain, all tides overflowing and dispensing with the decadent world, clearing the field for a new civilization. 'Creation destroys as it goes', he continues in *St Mawr*, 'throw[ing] down one tree for the rise of another' (*CSN* 342).

KNOWLEDGE AS DEATH

> So, there is nothing absolute left in the universe.... pure knowledge is only such a tiny bit of the universe, and always relative to the thing known and to the knower. (*FU* 181)

This debased world, which debilitates vitality so disastrously, takes many forms in Lawrence's work. It might be said that all objects of criticism in Lawrence are censured primarily because of their life-denying properties. The oft-repeated charge against cerebral knowledge is central to his censure of those elements of modern culture which challenge the primacy of life. We could tackle knowledge in several ways. First, in terms of Lawrence's specific diatribe against particular 'knowers' – Hermione Roddice, Miriam Lievers, Clifford Chatterley, a whole host of figures in the short stories. Second, through his positive celebration of life-charged 'blood-knowledge'. And finally, by thinking about an important contradiction – that Lawrence's critique of mental knowledge is often intimately bound up with his ambivalent relationship to Western culture, the Western culture of which he, himself, is a part.

Much of this comes down to his particular take on the mind/body distinction which, as we shall see, is more like a mind/mind distinction. 'At a certain point in his evolution, man became cognitively conscious', Lawrence writes in his 1927 review of Trigant Burrow's *The Social Basis of Consciousness*,

> he bit the apple: he began to know. Up till that time his consciousness flowed unaware, as in the animals. Suddenly, his consciousness split. (*P*1 378)

Knowledge is then at root *self*-knowledge ('Consciousness is self-consciousness', (*P*1 379)). In taking the self as its own object, the self becomes both object *and* subject, seer *and* seen in the same narcissistic process. This is partly that 'ego-binding' I mentioned earlier, but what interests me now is how self-consciousness also enacts a division, opens a gulf in the self. It is this division across the knower/known divide which first splits the self against itself, making the known self victim of the knower:

> Suddenly aware of himself, and of other selves over against him, man is a prey to the division inside himself. (*P*1 379)

Although this articulation is part of a wider plea to re-unify the separate elements of the self in an effort to take it 'beyond knowledge', it may be that finally it is this subjective division which most interests Lawrence, so much effort does he spend opening it up, dissecting, diagnosing.

As I have argued in *Sex in the Head,* this critique of mental knowledge focuses specifically on women, women who have had to stand as the fleshly apotheosis of Lawrence's bestiary of vices. 'Teach a woman to act from an idea', he writes in *Fantasia,* 'and you destroy her womanhood for ever. Make a woman self-conscious, and her soul is barren as a sandbag'. It was woman specifically and not mankind generally who brought mental knowledge into the world: 'When Eve ate that particular apple', he continues, 'she became aware of her womanhood, mentally'. The prime original sin thus affects woman, who 'is born with the disease of her own self-consciousness, as was her mother before her' (*FU* 85). 'Cocksure Women and Hensure Men', 'Women are so Cocksure', 'The "Jeune Fille" Wants to Know', 'Matriarchy', 'Give Her a Pattern' are all late essays which dig away at this sticky issue in various ways and underpin some of Lawrence's more controversial characterizations. 'Sex in the head' rather than in the blood is the contemporary extrapolation of the split in knowledge which took place when Eve ate the apple. Modern minds can only experience modern sex, as a bloodless, cerebrally driven, pornographic affair (and for Lawrence 'pornography' was always a dirty word, against which he defended his sexually explicit writings up to his death). Hermione Roddice in *Women in Love* is, in chapter 3 of the novel, bitterly demonized for wanting 'to have everything in [her] own volition, [her] deliberate voluntary consciousness'. Hermione is 'a *Kulturträger*, a medium for the culture of ideas', which is given to be a key symptom of personal deficiency: 'the pensive, tortured woman piled up her own defences of aesthetic knowledge, and culture, and world-visions and disinterestedness', in a desperate attempt to, as Lawrence puts it, 'stop up the terrible gap of insufficiency' (*WL* 63–4). Lady Ottoline Morrell, on whom the character is allegedly based, threatened to sue. As midwife rather than begetter of culture, Hermione bears the brunt of one of Lawrence's nastiest critiques. Birkin again articulates the knowledge split which has brought about this mental primacy, against Hermione the modern woman:

> Knowledge means everything to you. Even your animalism, you want it in your head. You don't want to *be* an animal, you want to observe your own animal functions, to get a mental thrill out of them. (*WL* 91)

He prescribes violence as cure:

> you want it all in that loathsome little skull of yours, that ought to be cracked like a nut.... If one cracked your skull perhaps one might get a spontaneous, passionate woman out of you, with real sensuality. As it is, what you want is pornography – looking at yourself in mirrors, watching your naked animal actions in mirrors, so that you can have it all in your consciousness, making it all mental. (*WL* 92)

Hermione is Eve, turning knowledge into a fetishized form of sex, making visual knowledge sexual. Knowledge of self and knowledge of sex are thus the result of the same primal crime: 'There is only one tree, there is only one fruit, in your mouth', rages Birkin, 'The eternal apple' (*WL* 89–90).

Against 'sex in the head' is set 'sex in the blood'. 'I carry a whole waste-paper basket of ideas at the top of my head', Lawrence writes in 'The Novel and the Feelings', 'and in some other part of my anatomy, the dark continent of myself' (*P*1 756). The abstract thought of philosophers, he writes in 'Why the Novel Matters', is only valued because the philosophers who do the thinking have said it must be so ('It is as if a rabbit, because he can make little pills, should decide that nothing but little pills matter', (*P*1 535)). Yet Lawrence's attempts to define other kinds of knowledge sometimes fare no better. When the baffled Hermione asks what knowledge 'not in your head' would be, she receives the full-blown Lawrentian response, spoken here by Birkin but developed elsewhere across Lawrence's work:

> In the blood... when the mind and the known world is drowned in darkness – everything must go – there must be the deluge. Then you find yourself a palpable body of darkness, a demon – (*WL* 92–3)

Perhaps this is arguing with a hammer. Mental knowledge is investigated in subtler ways elsewhere. Ursula in *The Rainbow* strikes out for an independence which is partly determined by her relationship to culture-as-knowledge: 'She wanted to read great, beautiful books, and be rich with them' (*R.* 406). This is duly undermined through the biting condemnation of formal education which follows, with Ursula positioned first as producer and dealer of knowledge in the awful struggle as a junior teacher, and then as its consumer when she becomes a student at Nottingham University. At first she regards the lecturers as 'black-gowned priests of knowledge': 'there was such freedom and pleasure in ranging over the very stuff of knowledge, and seeing how it moved and lived and had its being' (*R.* 431). But this changes – she idly looks out of her lecture-hall window and watches a woman walk by: 'In what world of reality was the woman in the pink dress walking? To what warehouse of dead unreality was she herself confined?' (*R.* 435) she muses (although this event is tackled rather more positively in Lawrence's early poem 'From a College Window', when the student sits above the world of work, 'absolved, assured I am better off/ Beyond a world I never want to join', (*Poems*, 36)). The college as a 'warehouse' is key here to Ursula's developing disillusionment. As she becomes bored and dissatisfied, knowledge emerges as seldom pure and always commercially interested. Latin becomes 'So much dry goods of knowledge'; the 'priests' mutate into mere middle-men marketing the exam skills needed for graduation to the workplace:

> it was a sham store, a sham warehouse, with a single motive of material gain, and no productivity. It pretended to exist by the religious virtue of knowledge. But the religious virtue of knowledge was become a flunkey to the god of material success. (*R.* 434–5)

Industrial materialism thus continues to underpin the litany of Lawrentian sins (he often fantasized about getting rid of money). What is 'wrong' with Hermione is mental possessiveness, the need to 'have', through consumption, nuggets of truth held fixed in-the-head. What is 'wrong' with University is, for Ursula, its role in the wider conveyor-belt of the marketplace. This critical context, of possessiveness and consumption, may get lost in Lawrence's later reveries in blood-consciousness. For the moment, I want to turn to the impact this has on Lawrence's thinking on culture and how we should approach it.

CULTURE AND MODERNISM

The choice seems to be simple: choose quickness not the corpse, choose vivid life over living death, choose blood- rather than mind-knowledge. Choose bodies over books, perhaps – choose sex not consciousness. But this is where these apparently clear-cut distinctions get messier; Lawrence does not always prefer nature over culture, body over intellect, animal over human, savage over social. Indeed, the paradoxical role of 'living' culture in this schema is a crucial element of tension in Lawrence's work. He, after all, chooses sex *in* books. Culture is writing too. Lawrence's critique is thus always partly a self-critique. When he battles with hedged-and-fenced 'diseased' Englishness, it is through an English sensibility. Humanity might mark the earth with 'eruptions', but it also writes books. Culture is as much the context and vehicle as the object of his critique. Lawrence is a writer whose deep suspicion of mental acts takes place *in* the text; the only 'body' these ideas have is the body *of* the text. Life, for Lawrence, inhabits and animates the book, the Word (and its embodiment in the novel as 'the one bright book of life' – 'Why the Novel Matters', (*P*1 535)), even if it is also betrayed by it.

How, then, does Lawrence regard the work that he does? And how does he represent culture in his writings? His writing about writing itself, and about cultural production, is closely linked to what he has to say about mental knowledge, how it is dispensed, how it is valued. Despite Ursula's student *ennui, The Rainbow* finally leaves open a space within which disinterested knowledge can still exist as a noble human pursuit. *Women in Love,* however, does not read knowledge as cultural object or artefact, or as mental control or process, quite so favourably. It is perhaps *the* novel of modernism which thrashes out most thoroughly the implications of what writing and the visual arts (particularly painting and sculpture) were trying to do during World War I. Lawrence himself was loosely connected with three key artistic groups when he was still working in Britain, the most famous being the Bloomsbury Group, which included writers E. M. Forster, Clive Bell and Virginia Woolf, philosopher Bertrand Russell, economist John Maynard Keynes, painters Duncan Grant and Vanessa Bell. Although he entered into an intense correspondence with Russell for a time, the 'Other Bloomsbury' formed around Lawrence. At the same time, Lawrence published poems in the Imagism collections edited by Ezra Pound, the first of which was *Des Imagistes* (1914). Although he could not finally be called an imagist in the sense that Pound or H.D. or T. E. Hulme were, nevertheless this linked him to the camp of imagism/vorticism, which also included artists Wyndham Lewis, Jacob Epstein, and Henri Gaudier-Brzeska.

Women in Love engages with questions thrown up by the conflicting emphases of these groups. Indeed, it stages a number of overlapping discussions between its own modernist allegiances; the novel as a whole is a melting-pot of ideas. The issues which have dominated critical discussion concern its complex of relationships and its analysis of art. In writing so explicitly about art in modernism, Lawrence is working on at least two levels. Discussion of culture doesn't just take place *within* the novel, but it is also the frame within which the novel can *think about itself* and its own role as a cultural artefact. The discussion of the primitive African carving of a woman in childbirth in chapters 6 and 7 is particularly important when set against Birkin's struggle to find himself 'a palpable body of darkness'. This is art which might match that, conveying 'the extreme of physical sensation, beyond the limits of mental consciousness' (*WL* 127).

This is part of a whole discussion running through *Women in Love*, which gradually unravels or dissects art's role in the life of a culture, an artist, a spectator or a reader. Perhaps the novel's most important artistic episode is that which takes place across its final scenes, between Gudrun and Loerke, who asserts that 'art should *interpret* industry'(*WL* 518). There is also the strange, modernistic little dance which Hermione, Ursula and the Contessa perform 'in the style of the Russian ballet of Pavlova and Nijinsky' (*WL* 147–8). Gudrun's art lesson with Gerald's young sister Winifred focuses on how to represent on paper the strange otherness of a non-human form, first a grotesque Pekinese dog called Looloo ('Let's...see if we can get his Looliness, shall we?'), then the mad rabbit Bismarck. The scene culminates in a frenzied, sado-masochistic struggle between Gudrun and Bismarck, watched over by Gerald as if it were an erotic spectacle. Lawrence frequently uses people's interactions with animals – Gerald beating his horse earlier in the novel, Lou

Witt and the horse St Mawr, the bullfight scene at the start of *The Plumed Serpent*, Mellors hatching the pheasant eggs in *Lady Chatterley's Lover* – as a frame or metaphor for thinking through people's interactions with people. The cockerel in 'The Escaped Cock', the fox in the story of that name, out-manning the farming women with its male cunning, Mino the tom-cat in *Women in Love*, overwhelming his female feline because of his anatomical disposition to dominance, are all male animals standing in for phallic men. Furthermore, Lawrence interrogates his own relationship to culture by showing his characters struggling to develop new artistic forms (like Gudrun, Paul Morel paints, whilst Siegmund in *The Trespasser* and Aaron Sisson are musicians). Animals function as the 'lively' objects who mediate this self- and cultural-analysis, as alternative forms of life who either stand full-square for the human interpreter's opinions or challenge his view by their radical difference. In his animal poems, especially those in *Birds, Beasts and Flowers*, Lawrence muses as much on his own position as reader, viewer, interpreter of animals, as on the creatures themselves. 'Fish' (*Poems*, 334–40) addresses the limits of human knowledge when apprehending another life-form:

> They are beyond me, are fishes.
> I stand at the pale of my being
> And look beyond, and see
> Fish, in the outerwards,
> As one stands on a bank and looks in.

In 'Tortoise Shout' (*Poems*, 363–7), animal-language is immediately translated into human:

> I thought he was dumb,
> I said he was dumb,
> Yet I've heard him cry....
> Worse than the cry of the new-born,
> A scream,
> A yell,
> A shout,
> A pæan,
> A death-agony,
> A birth-cry,
> A submission,
> A tiny, tiny, far away, reptile under the first dawn.

As it turns out, the cry is a mating-cry, which causes Lawrence to meditate on sex as generator of the voice, language and the spoken self:

> Sex, which breaks us into voice, sets us calling across the
> deeps, calling, calling for the complement,
> Singing, and calling, and singing again, being answered, having found.

In *Women in Love*, Looloo the dog, and later Bismarck the rabbit, become mediators of people's desire, and signs in a system which shows their difficult relationship to culture. As Winifred draws her dog, the artwork betrays what the artist cannot: she might cluck sentimentally about 'mummy draw[ing] its beautiful portrait', but what spills onto the page is 'a grotesque little diagram of a grotesque little animal, so wicked and so comical' (*WL* 310). Lawrence will happily slide into absurd anthropomorphism if it will make his phallic point, but here the dog seems to acquire some sort of integrity, as a very different kind of being, via Winifred's drawing. Never trust the artist, trust the tale.

READING AND THE NOVEL

Women in Love also slides around on the issue of *how* knowledge is produced, whether through a kind of cerebral violence, or as part of a more 'lively' or 'vivid' desire. It actively thinks about culture as consumption – about how we read, how we see, how we take in art as its recipients. Birkin copies a Chinese drawing of geese 'to know China' through it: 'One gets more of China, copying this picture, than reading all the books' (*WL* 145). This is Birkin as consumer of culture – as the 'knower' of China who gets to it through its artworks (it is also another animal-image mediating a human's relationship to culture, and other cultures). Birkin becomes a knowing, and participating, critic through a visual engagement. Hermione, whose 'will to know' had earlier been subject to such a savage castigation, argues in chapter 12 *against* knowing as possession (as, indeed, she had been trying to do in the earlier passage I discussed, though Birkin was unwilling to let her get a word in edgeways). Now, debating with Ursula over the 'poking and prying' of knowledge-gathering, the need to realize things 'in the head', she asks, 'don't you feel you *can't* be tortured into any more knowledge?' (*WL* 203). Briefly, it becomes Birkin who, for Hermione at least, 'murders to dissect': 'He really is like a boy who must pull everything to pieces to see how it is made', to which Ursula replies, 'Like tearing open a bud to see what the flower will be like' (*WL* 204).

Elsewhere Lawrence returns to this, thinking about what this would mean for books as well as flowers. *Apocalypse* (written in the last year of Lawrence's life) is a literary-critical investigation of the power of writing. Part of Lawrence's quarrel with Christianity is his objection to the death of its book, the Bible. Christianity is dead because its text is. Writing here is explicitly given an organic identity, for writing, like other natural forms, can be killed if it is not read or used in the right way. The text of Christianity was thus killed by its readers:

> Now a book lives as long as it is unfathomed. Once it is fathomed, it dies at once.... Once a book is fathomed, once it is *known*, and its meaning is fixed and established, it is dead. (*A.* 4)

Just as Birkin's murderous 'knowledge' of the bud stops it becoming a flower, so Christianity's need to fix the meanings of its text has killed the text, and all hope of it ever meaning anything again. 'Fathoming' thus takes place whenever one would know beyond doubt. Knowledge fixes, and the fixed thing cannot move.

This 'fathoming' is also what Lawrence sees at work in psychoanalysis (which is why he argues against it so vehemently). In his understanding of Freudianism, theory is applied to 'text' (whether the text is a book or the unspoolings of the subject's unconscious), and it is theory which dictates what the Freudian will find. '"Theory as theory" is all right', he writes in the review of Burrow's *Social Basis of Consciousness* (and he should know – he does enough of it himself),

> But the moment you apply it to life, especially to the subjective life, the theory becomes mechanistic, a substitute for life, a factor in the vicious unconscious. So that while the Freudian theory of the unconscious and of the incest-motive is valuable as a description of our psychological condition, the moment you begin to apply it, and make it master of the living situation, you have begun to substitute one mechanistic or unconscious illusion for another. (*P*1 378)

Finding what you are looking for in your object is the problem here, risking killing off elements which may surprise you or contradict your model by imposing prescribed limits on your findings. In this sense, Lawrence's image of what a Freudian reading is – whether it is of a cultural object, or of an individual psyche – is simply another incarnation of the process which had already been used in Christian interpretation, with the unconscious rather than God as the truth-to-be-found, the knowledge-to-be-had. Psychoanalysis looks for something in a way which ensures that it will find it. Christianity too can brook no contradiction:

> The interpretation was always the same, whether it was a Doctor of Divinity in the pulpit, or the big blacksmith who was my Sunday-school teacher. Not only was the Bible verbally trodden into the consciousness, like innumerable foot-prints treading a surface hard, but the foot-prints were always mechanically alike, the interpretation was fixed, so that all real interest was lost. (*A.* 4)

This is an extraordinary moment in Lawrence, which needs to be looked at not just in the context of the critique of organized religion which is taking place throughout *Apocalypse*, but as a more general statement about reading itself, about critical activity, about the reader's or viewer's engagement with culture's objects. What kills the book is the reader, whose desire to pin its meaning down to something fixed and known limits it for ever. He continues:

> A book only lives while it has the power to move us, and move us *differently*; so long as we find it *different* every time we read it.

Writing to Edward Garnett as *The Sisters* was developing, Lawrence asserted that *he too* now 'had to write differently'. Writing differently also means reading differently, and what Lawrence advocates in *Apocalypse* is a form of reading which will always find difference in the text. Again, this is threaded through with a militant anti-consumerism, as Lawrence champions cultural experience which is not about accumulating knowledge but experiencing otherness. 'Value' here becomes an aesthetic rather than a commercial category:

> we are so overwhelmed with quantities of books, that we hardly realize any more that a book can be valuable, valuable like a jewel, or

> a lovely picture, into which you can look deeper and deeper and get a more profound experience every time. Far better to read one book six times, at intervals, than to read six several books. (*A*. 4–5)

Clearly there is some element of writerly self-interest at work here, with Lawrence suggesting that *his* books, too, are those valuable objects which must be returned to, repeatedly moving us 'differently'. It is also perhaps a warning to the critic who would 'know' the text (Lawrence's text), who would kill its meaning and pin it down, to take care with Lawrence's own work. He sees the fact that *Apocalypse* is 'not what the vulgar public calls "readable"' as a virtue ('It is very fragmentary ... But in fragments fascinating' (*L7*, 507). Vulgar readers, with their vulgar critical intentions, should beware.

The unfinished novel *Mr Noon* is peppered with diatribes against a presumed 'dear reader' who, the narrator expects, will try to 'pin the novel down' but will ultimately find nothing:

> Therefore you sniffling mongrel-bitch of a reader, you can't sniff out any specific why or any specific wherefore, with your carrion-smelling psycho-analysing nose, because there *is* no why and wherefore. (*MN* 205)

Vicious as this sounds, it needs to be read in the context of some of Lawrence's non-fictional critical statements about novels, most importantly 'Surgery for the Novel – or a Bomb' (1923), 'The Novel', 'Morality and the Novel', 'Why the Novel Matters' (all 1925), as well as 'The Novel and the Feelings', which I have already mentioned. '[A] work of art is an act of faith', he wrote; 'one goes on writing, to the unseen witnesses'. There is a vulnerability in the desperation with which Lawrence occasionally bullies his readers into the right response, trying to guarantee that we will trust the artist *rather than* our own reading of the tale. Or perhaps he would simply like to ensure that his own works have a more open textual future than the Bible? The one point to which the Novel essays keep returning is that this is a form which is 'incapable of the absolute' ('The Novel', *P2* 416) – ironic, since it is this issue which shows Lawrence at *his* most absolute, at *his* most didactic. Novels are open to messiness, contradiction, relativity, and because of this Lawrence was more committed to them than any other form:

> Now in a novel there's always a tom-cat, a black tom-cat that pounces

> on the white dove of the Word, if the dove doesn't watch it; and there is a banana-skin to trip on; and you know there is a water-closet on the premises. (*P*2 418)

This is the novel's 'life', this is why for Lawrence it is 'the one bright book of life'. Novels 'wont *let* you tell didactic lies'.

> If you try to nail anything down, in the novel, either it kills the novel, or the novel gets up and walks away with the nail. ('Morality and the Novel', *P*1 528)

The idea is developed much more fully in 'Why the Novel Matters', where Lawrence's advocacy of life, and his celebration of (his idea of) the novel, come together in an image of the character read differently:

> In the novel, the characters can do nothing but *live*. If they keep on being good, according to pattern, or bad, according to pattern, or even volatile, according to pattern, they cease to live, and the novel falls dead. A character in a novel has got to live, or it is nothing.
>
> We, likewise, in life have got to live, or we are nothing. (*P*1 537)

Perhaps this says more about Lawrence's discourse of vividness than the history of the novel. Certainly, this is what he was trying to do in his own work, and it is why, though he wrote in every form available to him, the novel was his preferred mode. This is partly because, for him, it has the power to disrupt conscious or intellectual primacy, set the wild things free, speak the unspeakable. But he is also clearly aware of his writing as a form of exchange (or else why would he be so worried about his implied reader and her critical pin?), and here we should begin to think about novels as sites of challenge on a number of levels – challenging the character with difference, exposing the novelist as 'a dribbling liar' and speaking despite him, confronting the reader with an experience of the other:

> If we can't hear the cries far down in our own forests of dark veins, we can look in the real novels, and there listen-in. Not listen to the didactic statements of the author, but to the low, calling cries of the characters, as they wander in the dark woods of their destiny. ('The Novel and the Feelings' *P*1 759–60)

Writing thus has the power to disrupt the reader's sense of self, but only if she reads 'openly', not pinning down the text, not requiring it to conform to a fixed pattern. One reason why

Lawrence scholars have been traditionally so 'anti-theory' (by which is meant opposed to the philosophically or psychoanalytically informed theories of culture and subject which precipitated the so-called 'Crisis in English Studies' in the 1970s and 1980s), is that they have taken this Lawrentian opposition to a pre-ordained pattern as itself a critique of models of reading which will determine the limits of the text. To have a theory of reading, or of writing, was like stating in advance of opening the book that you knew what you were supposed to find, and so could *ensure* that those 'mechanical foot-prints' would be 'always alike', nailing down the novel, boxing up the black tom-cat. Of course, Lawrence's call to difference, to open readings – a call answered by 'the low calling cries' of the text's difference, its IT, its contradictoriness – is itself highly theorized. And it is precisely those new theories of the subject, of sex, and of text, which have allowed us to 'burst the bound hide' of Leavisite personal response – a fixed pattern for reading if ever there was one. It is not, then, just the novels themselves which are moving away from 'the old stable ego of the character'. For Lawrence writing can also move the reader away from her stability, into difference. For writer, reader and character, the cultural experience of the novel must be troubled, provocative, discomforting.

I began this chapter by thinking about Lawrence's positive terms – life, quickness, the 'IT' – then worked through a number of negative definitions – the industrial, commercial, cerebral self as incompatible with, as the contradiction of, 'vivid' man. We have still to explore the pristine body, and its quickness, but now I want to examine in more detail how Lawrence develops his 'writing otherwise' by exploding the stable ego further, looking closely at his exploration of home and homelessness.

2

Family Romances: Home, marriage and memory

Lawrence's selves are borne of their desire, and their struggle is to wrest control of that desire, to fulfil and keep faith with it: possession of 'one's own soul in silence' is the ultimate tenet of Lawrence's individualism. But Lawrence's selves are also borne into intense human webs, demanding nets of need and dependence, which curtail and contain that desire. A double current runs through and animates the self here, a tension between urgent, individual desire and the frame which holds it in check. This is what I want to explore in this chapter.

Throwing his actors into an inevitable social connectedness, Lawrence insistently challenges their sovereignty by trial of family and community. The struggles of the individual for self-contained isolation, such as those described in 'The Man Who Loved Islands', 'The Escaped Cock', and 'The Man Who Was Through with the World', are futile. The family immerses the subject in the social. Perhaps even more than the antihumanist IT or unconscious which I discussed earlier, the family is the most visible stage upon which the 'old stable ego' is challenged. 'What must be broken is the egocentric absolute of the individual', Lawrence writes in his review of Burrow's *Social Basis of Consciousness*:

> We are all such hopeless little absolutes to ourselves. And if we are sensitive, it hurts us, and we complain, we are called neurotic. If we are complacent, we enjoy our own petty absolutism though we hide it and pretend to be quite meek and humble. But in secret, we are absolute and perfect to ourselves, and nobody could be better than we are. This is called being normal. (*P*1 379)

In Lawrence, no one is normal. The narcissistic ego cannot reign absolute for long when subjected to the unremitting challenge of context. This, then, is what relativity means to Lawrence: although as I said earlier he occasionally laments the fact that there is no longer 'one absolute principle in the universe', relativity ensures that his individuals are never allowed to be absolute and complete for and in themselves. His dramas of subjectivity are staged in a way which inevitably undercuts the sovereignty of the subject. 'I think everything is relative', he writes in *Fantasia of the Unconscious*,

> But I also feel, most strongly, that in itself each individual living creature is absolute: in its own being. And that all things in the universe are just relative to this individual living creature. And that individual living creatures are relative to each other. (*FU* 182)

The most significant site of this struggle is the home. At home Lawrence's individual grapples to be himself (for 'he' is usually a he, and the opponent in this struggle, desire's impediment is mother, wife, child). But 'home' is also the place where desire comes to be, as well as the place where it is dashed, shaped, checked. Caught in the effort to extract themselves from the domestic mesh, or else striving to produce an alternative community not based on blood-ties, Lawrence's characters have a keen sense of the social, of themselves embedded within the social. Of course 'home' in Lawrence also means more than the domestic space, encompassing one's cultural or national origin – Englishness, Lawrence's specific 'Spirit of Place', the language one writes in, the place one grew up in. Coming to terms with and constructing a response to this wider understanding of 'home' is a crucial tension in Lawrence's work. His novels repeatedly call for a reconfiguration of relationships cut to the measure of desire – not convention, or legally binding contracts of love, or family responsibility. He both celebrates and rejects the family. If the classic novel ends with marriage and familial consensus, Lawrence's end with questions, break-ups, suicides and equivocation.

Both men and women fare differently in this set-up. Sexual consummation may well be the primal organizing principle of Lawrence's universe (as I will explore in chapter 4), but anatomy is not destiny. A woman's fulfilment is not found in childbirth; her struggle is an adult struggle with other adults. Like

Lawrence's men, she battles in the workplace, she travels, she fights, she refuses, she finds sexual pleasure. There is, of course, another story to be told here, and feminism has traced it eloquently: Lawrence's women may be freed from the constraints of home as destiny, but Lawrence also argues for their final submission to an overarching masculinity. Their struggle and surrender – and pleasure – generally takes place in a heterosexual union within which woman is charged to obey. That these women submit only partially, and with great resistance, is central to Lawrence's interest in them as divided subjects, and crucial to how we read his misogyny.

EXCLUDED FATHERS AND ABJECT MOTHERS

The central relationships of Lawrence's tales are edgy unions which take place at the margins. Secret adulteries, a struggle to forge non-conventional marriages against the grain of social code, a refusal to set 'ideal' unions in a domestic context: this is how Lawrence confronts changes in what men and women want. *The Trespasser* explores adultery. In *Sons and Lovers* Paul's struggle for his lovers is marred by his relationship with his mother, herself trapped in a disastrous marriage. In *The Rainbow* Ursula refuses marriage and then miscarries. In *Women in Love* she tries to recast marriage as a radical act, and ends up sharing her husband with a man. Gerald's relationship failures cause him to commit suicide, an act prefigured by Siegmund in *The Trespasser*. The *Lady Chatterley* novels famously focus on an aristocratic woman leaving her husband for one of the servants. If each of these texts strives to find an open context for desire, they do so by dramatizing the destruction of the traditional spaces in which desire could only partially be expressed: conventional marriage, domestic confinement, sex linked to procreation.

This breakdown positions men and women differently. Male desire in Lawrence, far from governing the family castle, is increasingly excluded. Two scenes of errant husbands leaving their families, first in *The Trespasser* and then again in *Aaron's Rod*, figure the man outside, excluded from the family nest and the intimacy of woman and children. In the later novel, Aaron watches the spectacle of domesticity from the other side of the window, a nefarious Peeping Tom guiltily perusing the scene of his exclusion, watching wife and daughters go about their business unaware that they are on view. In her feminist reading, Sheila MacLeod analyses the one-sidedness of the scene as very obviously one of *female*, not male, exclusion:

> The beginning of *Aaron's Rod*, where Aaron walks out on his wife and children just before Christmas, enraged and frightened me to an extent I would not have been able to admit. I didn't want to know what happened to Aaron. I wanted to know what happened to Lottie Sisson without her husband and to Millicent and Marjory without their father. It was as if Lawrence had wiped them out, relegated them to some sub-world not worth writing about.[1]

Certainly this response is warranted since Aaron's is the novel's point of view, and those private folk on the inside are not the story's heart. But point of view here is set up from the start as that of the outsider, the stranger – of masculinity beyond the margins of the privileged domestic space.

In *The Trespasser*, a novel whose very title signals the illicit relationship as an act of law-breaking, when the intrusive lover enters and breaks open terrain she does not own, it is Siegmund who is excluded, and who reacts with an extraordinary explosion of defensive repulsion. Returning home after mother and children have gone to bed, he moves through the house, on the eve of his holiday with his lover Helena, and finds that he has already left:

> As he watched them, he hated the children, for being so dear to him. Either he himself must go under, and drag on an existence he hated, or they must suffer. But he had agreed to spend this holiday with Helena, and meant to do so. As he turned, he saw himself like a ghost cross the mirror. He looked back; he peered at himself. (*T.* 51)

Far from ruling the roost, this father barely haunts it – later in the novel he calls himself 'a family criminal' (*T.* 174). This passage is preceded by a long judgemental survey of the 'drab and dreary' terrain of the domestic woman, which is contrasted with later images of the 'clean' free spirit Helena, whose whiteness and sparkle is reiterated, even though she is the story's nominal scarlet woman and ought to be socially 'dirtied' by her 'trespass', by her role in Siegmund's adultery. Lawrence does not bother to investigate the politics of domestic drudgery nor the difficulty of raising children. Instead, he deploys the opposition of disease and health, dirt and cleanliness, in service of a specific domestic conflict, to justify Siegmund's choice of the fresh, free Helena over the grimy family landscape.

Motherhood in *The Trespasser* is almost entirely figured through the abjection of litter, the signs of bodily chaos and disarray which are left when mother and daughters have gone to bed. If cleanliness is next to godliness (as the old British saying runs), then Beatrice, Siegmund's slatternly wife, has practically blasphemed in failing as a housekeeper (this is actually only one moment in a long critique of women who fail in their domestic duties; in *Fantasia of the Unconscious* Lawrence even prescribes learning 'the domestic arts' as a cure for female narcissism). The two paragraphs which follow the sentence 'As [Siegmund] lay in his arm-chair he looked round with disgust' (*T.* 50) are crafted on the classic lines of Julia Kristeva's analysis of the mother's body as a site of abjection and disgust in *Powers of Horror*. Although the mother (Beatrice) is not present, we have to read his repulsion as horror that she and her daughterly appendages have infected the whole house, that the house has become the externalization of the female domestic body. The stains and the dirt (repeated words) are metonyms of this body: the dirty cloth 'had great brown stains betokening children', and the stain on Siegmund's chipped mug 'had gone under the glaze, so that it looked like the mark of a dirty mouth' (*T.* 50). Wear and tear on floor and furniture tells the history of fleshly contact; scattered objects are signs of eating, play and decay (ash, sweets, flies, 'crusts of bread, and crusts of bread and jam').

Pernicious as this may be, it is part of an ongoing discussion of masculinity and the home which runs through Lawrence's work. The figure of the excluded father focuses his anxiety about men's role, women's primacy, and the inability of the family to contain sexual desire. Yet elsewhere – Lawrence's next novel, in fact – home is the space of cultural acquisition: pristine and ordered, intellectually challenging, the domain of exquisite intimacy between mother and son. In *Sons and Lovers* the abjection of *The Trespasser* becomes cosy, uncomfortably comfortable intimacy. Beatrice is condemned partly because, within her domestic space, the boundaries between the maternal body and the home itself have become blurred. She is also condemned because she is one type of mother, not another. Siegmund finds himself sitting on a comb, which becomes a sign of his life with her, as well as her laxity: 'This was the summary of his domestic life: a broken, coarse comb, a child crying because her hair was tugged, a wife who had let the hair go till now, when she had got into a temper to see the job through' (*T.* 51).

Contrast this with *Sons and Lovers*, and with the preferred maternalism of Mrs Morel, the good mother. Certainly, this is another novel of fatherly alienation, but this time played out from the other side, as mother and children band together in a union of loyalty staged in the spick and span domesticity of Mrs Morel's home, and pitted against the drunken, dirty father. In *The Trespasser*, when Siegmund returns from his holiday with Helena it is he – father and husband – who waits upstairs, listening to the sounds of the family which has left him out of their intimacies. In *Sons and Lovers*, we listen with the children from their bedroom as they suffer through the arguments of their parents. The move from *The Trespasser* to *Sons and Lovers* is partly a move from the father's to the son's point of view. As father, Mr Morel's exclusion in the latter novel has been read as a necessary part of the Oedipal drama which unfolds between mother and son. In all this, the father comes off rather badly, his prime role that of rival in love. Later in life, when physical, earthy masculinity had taken a more central place in his agenda, Lawrence claimed to regret the novel's largely negative casting of the natural, if ruined, Morel as the novel's bullying spirit of disruption. And in a notorious chapter ('Parent Love') in *Fantasia of the Unconscious*, Lawrence also engages in a lengthy critique of the indulgent mother 'with her boy of eighteen', a passage which needs to be set alongside the more intimate moments of Oedipal desire which pass between Paul and his mother in the earlier novel. Here the mother, 'diseased with self-consciousness and sex in the head',

> beats about for her insatiable satisfaction, seeking whom she may devour. And usually, she turns to her child. Here she provokes what she wants. . . . So she throws herself into a last great love for her son, a final and fatal devotion, that which would have been the richness and strength of her husband and is poison to the boy. (*FU* 125)

Lawrence's discourse on the ruptured modern family is thus inconsistent, and he is not afraid to open up its dangers and disturbances. Both Morel and Siegmund love their children despite their estrangement; like Lawrence's later silent but passionate heroes, Morel, in particular, loves but cannot articulate that love, and inhabits a world (fashioned by the educated woman) where the control of words is paramount. Mr Morel is a classic alienated, pre-new-man father: with no obvious role in the central activity of the home, financially central to the family unit but emotionally excluded from it, the nominally controlling patriarch finds himself domestically impotent. The male subject is increasingly fractured, and this break begins with the family itself.

There is an argument which could be made here for Lawrence as writer of proto-*Iron John* fables of the disenfranchised modern man: in 'Nottingham and the Mining Countryside', he writes that 'The men of England, the colliers in particular, are disheartened. They have been betrayed and beaten' (*P*1 137). In the central discussion of the family in *Fantasia of the Unconscious*, Lawrence actively advocates the absent-presence of the father, who might pass through the child's life but takes no responsibility for it. Although 'the child needs more than the mother. It needs as well the presence of men, the vibration from the present body of man', nevertheless 'the true male instinct is to avoid physical contact with a baby...present or absent, there should be between the baby and the father that strange, intangible communication', (*FU* 32–3). 'Intangible communication' is far from the litter and crusts which form the material bond between the unfortunate Beatrice and her daughters. But what unites these two unsympathetic views of the male role inside or rather outside of the family is the refusal of both to resurrect a traditional model of male domestic government. Lawrence's family structures are at best disaffected, at worse dysfunctional, with the father as well as the mother as focus of dissent and change. For if the father cannot control 'his' space, if his home is not his castle (in 1929 Lawrence writes that the working man's 'one desire is to get out of [his] "castle" and [his] "own little home"' (*P*1 138)), if his only real power is the power to leave (with his mistress or just down to the pub), then his position as seat of authority is fundamentally undermined.

Morel rants and rages against his domestic impotence, he tries to resurrect his control through violence, but this only makes resistance stronger. Certainly the father's power to absent himself is more than the women have, but they are always assured the loyalty of their children, and this essential bodily connection is elsewhere figured by Lawrence as a more than ample compensation.

'A CORRESPONDENCE OF BLOOD': MARRIAGE AND MATERNITY

What is remarkable about all this is not just that Lawrence's fathers fail to shore up their families under their control, nor that his mothers are dissatisfied with their lot, but that no one seems to be terribly interested in returning to the traditional image of the nuclear or extended family unit upheld by patriarchal law. If the Victorian ideal has turned dysfunctional, Lawrence will not lament, regret or try to glue it back together. Across his work he posits a number of alternative loose 'family' alliances based on choice and desire, not convention and law. Along with the death of god and the integrated rational subject goes that of the traditional domestic unit; Lawrence answers each of these losses by representing different experimental possibilities.

The ways in which the family, and the traditions of relationships it oversees, break down in Lawrence are diverse. After Siegmund's death in *The Trespasser* Beatrice moves house and follows her desire: she 'had had all her life a fancy for a more open, public form of living than that of a domestic circle' (*T.* 218). Often this is figured geographically: Canada beckons as a wide-open-space of possibility for relationships as well as work – Siegmund thinks of going there towards the end of *The Trespasser*, Connie and Mellors plan to flee to British Columbia at the end of *Lady Chatterley's Lover*, March and Henry await the boat across the Atlantic at the end of *The Fox*. Earlier I suggested that the fact that Lawrence distinguishes between a woman's life and her role as mother might constitute a liberation from the 'anatomy is destiny' model of innate femininity. In *The Rainbow*, as with the earlier novels, Anna's pregnancy and childbearing exclude Will, but Ursula's pregnancy fails. Her 'happy ending' is not marriage to Skrebensky, but independent self-discovery; the novel does not close with an image of patriarchal fulfilment or promised maternalism but with the suggestion that her putative individuality will survive. *Sons and Lovers* sees the failure as well as the development of at least four love affairs. Mr and Mrs Morel's starts with a marriage, but this signals the beginning of the breakdown of their love. William's relationship with Gypsy is doomed, as is he, partly because the two are *too* gender stereotyped, and he cannot bear the burden of her dependence. Paul's relationships with both Miriam and Clara fail because of his devotion to his mother. Only Clara follows a conventional path: after her affair with Paul, she returns to her husband, turns away from suffragism and back to traditional femininity. Paul finally leaves the family unit, but only with difficulty and after the death of his mother – and arguably only in the novel's final sentence. Indeed, it is his inability to tear himself away which is the main problem of the novel. Perhaps more than Clara and Paul's sexual consummation, readers bring away with them the Morel's violent struggles, one resulting in the wife's communing with lilies in the back garden after her husband has thrown her out. The early poem 'Discord in Childhood' articulates this from the listening child's point of view, as human violence echoes the shrieking of the wind in the ash-tree:

> Within the house two voices arose, a slender lash
> Whistling she-delirious rage, and the dreadful sound
> Of a male thong booming and bruising, until it had drowned
> The other voice in a silence of blood, 'neath the noise of the ash.
>
> (*Poems*, 36)

Conflict is endemic. In the later novels it is women who leave most readily. In *Women in Love*, Ursula and Gudrun's struggle with their father is also a struggle about changing class, for class, too, is 'home'. They leave, Ursula into marriage with Birkin, but a radical and loosely bisexual form of marriage which incorporates intense same-sex relationships too. This fails with Gerald's suicide and the couple's final inability to agree, but still the novel should be seen as a serious working-through of alternatives. Chapter 19, in which Birkin makes an absurd attempt to ask Ursula's father for her hand in marriage, is perhaps Lawrence's strongest argument against the institution in its traditional form:

'If one repents being married, the marriage is at an end', Birkin states to the older man. Earlier he had advocated marriage as only justifiable if it is a 'mystical conjunction': 'It is disgusting, people marrying for a home' (*WL* 215). In *Aaron's Rod*, Lilly, who seems to meet up with his wife Tanny infrequently and at different places across the globe, criticizes marriage as '*Egoisme à deux*': 'Two people, one egoism, Marriage is a self-conscious egoistic state' (*AR* 122). Much later, *Lady Chatterley's Lover* traces the breakdown of a sexless marriage and the development of a new form of relationship based on desire. At the end of the novel, however, Connie does *not* marry Mellors, although she is pregnant with his child. There is a promise of an alternative form of domestic bliss, but the two are apart, and can only write to each other, as if, finally, theirs is a connection which can only exist as text. Particularly in his writing up to the end of World War I, Lawrence shows himself to be quite aware of the restrictions which domesticity placed on women. Lydia Lensky mulls over the limitations of her first marriage in chapter 9 of *The Rainbow*, and on the first page of *Women in Love* Ursula quips in response to Gudrun's suggestion that marriage is 'bound to be an experience of some sort', 'Not really…More likely to be the end of experience'.

Of course Lawrence himself married, after eloping with an already married woman, and was passionately committed to marriage as 'a correspondence of blood'. Later in *Women in Love*, man's 'perfect union with a woman – sort of ultimate marriage' is seen as the highest ideal, 'seeing there's no God' (*WL* 64). Marriage as life-infused heterosexual connection rather than legal institution was for him 'the clue to human life, but there is no marriage apart from the wheeling sun and the nodding earth, from the straying of the planets and magnificence of the fixed stars' (not by any means a conventional description of the institution, especially coming from Lawrence's defensive polemic in justification of a novel about adultery, '*A Propos* of *Lady Chatterley's Lover*', (*P2* 504)). In 1917 he considered calling a collection of his verse 'Poems of a Married Man'. Soon after the elopement with Frieda, he wrote in a letter: 'Frieda and I have struggled through some bad times into a wonderful naked intimacy…I do love, and I am loved – I have given and I have taken – and that is eternal. Oh, if only people could marry properly, I believe in marriage' (*L*1 441). It must be said, however, that this was written some two years *before* Lawrence actually entered Kensington Registry Office and married Frieda officially.

More importantly, this connectedness is only fleetingly possible in Lawrence's narratives, which focus rather on disconnection than essential unity. When Kate Leslie in *The Plumed Serpent* leaves off being a solitary wanderer to marry, it is hardly a conventionally Christian affair, being the union of Kate, transformed by the act into the earthly embodiment of the Goddess Malintzi, and Cipriano, earthly representative of the God Huitzilopochtli, in the religion of Quetzalcoatl. Yet for all its outrageous authoritarianism and sexism, the novel ends with Kate's dissent and prevarication, and her aloofness from marriage, divine or not. Written at the same time as *The Plumed Serpent*, the notorious story 'The Woman Who Rode Away' may be the apotheosis of patriarchal sadism and control (I shall debate this in chapter 4), but it also figures a woman leaving her husband and son, who have never satisfied her, to find something different. It has been argued that since Lawrence probably could not have children, and since he certainly resented Frieda's relationship with hers (she had left and lost them when she eloped), then Lawrence would deny in print women's own satisfaction in motherhood. Persuasive as this may be, the counter-argument that at least this liberates his women from one form of biological determinism must also be considered. Of course, Anna Brangwen's exultation in her fertility in *The Rainbow*, and Mrs Morel's good mothering, might be cited against this argument too. But Mrs Morel is a figure of perverse control as well as domestic security, and *The Rainbow* enacts its own critique of women as mothers. The adolescent Ursula is the focus for this, animated by the double response of repulsion at her mother's overwhelming fertility and an urgent desire to enter the world of work. Her restlessness thus manifests itself as a rebellion against compulsory maternity, but a familiarly sexist instinct causes Lawrence to set Ursula's longing in the context of a struggle between women, when Anna, the scorning and jealous mother, undermines her daughter 'with all the cunning instinct of a breeding animal'. Ursula is provoked to revolt (in both senses of the word) against the abjection of maternity in a way which is remarkably similar to Siegmund's earlier reaction. Anna

> went about, big with child, slovenly, easy, having a certain lax dignity, taking her own time, pleasing herself, always, always doing things for the children, and feeling that she thereby fulfilled the whole of womanhood. (*R.* 354)

It is too much for Ursula who, insisting 'on the right of women to take equal place with men in the field of action and work', fights 'against the close, physical, limited life of herded domesticity' (*R.* 354). Yet mothers seldom win in Lawrence, and Ursula – through her rejection in *The Rainbow* and then through the role she plays in forming new networks in *Women in Love* – is an important switch-point in Lawrence's work.

FAMILY IN *THE RAINBOW*

Lawrence spends an inordinate amount of time sketching out domestic scenarios and then watching them crumble, although it is also true that his most characteristic *mise en scène* features the struggle of unrelated adults, the tension of friendship, the anxiety of sexuality between lovers wilfully negotiating each other's conflicting desire in the battle for equality, desperately passing the power back and forth. If marriage is foremost, friendship comes a close second: Gerald and Birkin in *Women in Love*, Aaron and Lilly in *Aaron's Rod*, Kangaroo and Somers in *Kangaroo*, Ramón and Cipriano in *The Plumed Serpent*, March and Banford in *The Fox*. Even Gudrun and Ursula emerge more clearly as best friends than as sisters (reading *Women in Love* I sometimes forget that they are related), and in *Sons and Lovers* Paul and Miriam are platonic friends before they ever become lovers. Add to this those key group-scenes which crystallize the issues of the novels – the discussion of the African statue in *Women in Love* between Gerald, Birkin and Halliday's bohemian friends; the discussion of love and Bolshevism early in *Lady Chatterley's Lover*; endless discussions of religion, race and politics in *The Plumed Serpent*: chapters called 'Talk' and 'Words' in *Aaron's Rod* – and we might say that the group which forms the key melting-pot of ideas and of subjective and social development in later Lawrence is that of friends, of equals, not of relatives. It is often said that real people simply 'don't talk like that': trying to understand Minette's dislike of black beetles, for instance, Gerald says 'Are you afraid of their biting, or is it a metaphysical antipathy?' (*WL* 123). This only seems unlikely or contrived if we want to read Gerald or Minette as identifiably human, as people on the page who are really just like us, descendants in a realist tradition of believable human figures. It might, however, be easier to read the characters who drift through *Women in Love* as agents of debate rather than as credible realist characters. Breakdown of the family unit as a unit of meaning is part of Lawrence's break with classic realism. It is the peer group, generally talking philosophy, culture, ideas, which comes to dominate Lawrence's narrative space, at the expense of the domestic hearth.

The Rainbow as a whole arguably charts this change of emphasis in Lawrence's mapping of relationships, from the moment at which the novel's first real family unit comes into being with the marriage of Tom and Lydia, to Ursula's independence and rejection of domesticity at the end. Lydia is an outsider who already has a child, Anna, by her first, now dead, husband. Tom becomes deeply attached to the child, but initially drifts apart from his wife. However, 'after two years of married life' their union is fully consummated in the true Lawrentian 'dark' sense, following an argument. In three brief pages in chapter 3, Tom and Lydia move from hostility, distance, seething chaos, to a recognition of each other's misery and loneliness which takes place through an experience of crossing over to see as the other sees. If, in Lawrence's 'power' period, conflicts are resolved through the assertion of will which results in one side's submission, here something like genuine empathy takes place, and this exchange of perspectives breaks down the terms of Tom and Lydia's struggle.

The meeting has profound implications for Anna, Lydia's little daughter (who is to become Ursula's mother, and focus, later in the novel, of the rebellion we saw above):

> Anna's soul was put at peace between them. She looked from one to the other, and she saw them established to her safety, and she was free. . . . She was no longer called upon to uphold with her childish might the broken end of the arch. Her father and her mother now met to the span of the heavens, and she, the child, was free to play in the space beneath, between. (*R.* 97)

Perhaps what is so moving about this is how simply it sketches out the architecture of security: home is the space to be 'free to play', home is the context which enables the child not to fret, not to take on a burden beyond her. The walls will not fall, and she can be confident. Home is then constraint, but it is only in its context that freedom ('play') can be experienced. Freedom, Lawrence writes in 'The Spirit of Place', is relative, subject to check, dependent on the boundaries of home and homeland. It has nothing to do with whether one feels free: the fulfilled self needs the context of community:

> men are free when they belong to a living, organic, *believing* community, active in fulfilling some unfulfilled, perhaps unrealised purpose....
>
> Men are not free when they are doing just what they like. The moment you can do just what you like, there is nothing you care about doing. (*SCAL* 12–13)

Of course, Lawrence is here talking about home in its widest sense ('Men are free when they are living in a homeland', he writes), but the principle is the same. The arch under which Anna plays is a similar constraint which enables freedom.

There are then two experiences of home here: home as the canopy for the child's development, the space which forges the growing subject – home perceived from the child's point of view. And there is the space which is carved out of the man and woman's desire. Lydia and Tom are certainly the context of Anna's security, but her experience of home and theirs is different. Anna is the child, Lydia and Tom the lovers. A result of their love is Anna's security, but their parenting seems almost accidental – only the effect of their bond as lovers. The generational story of *The Rainbow* is clearly centrally concerned with begetting and family history, but the focus of the narrative shifts as soon as possible to the child's experience of the family. At first this is Anna's; then, after Anna has become Will's lover and Ursula's mother, the childish point of view is Ursula's. Lawrence, then, can write as a lover, and he can write as a child, but it may be that his position on parenting is less sure. Certainly Mrs Morel's connection to her children is finely worked, but it is as overbearing as it is nurturing. And always – especially after *Sons and Lovers* – the intense feeling of parent for child is tinged with Oedipal conflict. In chapter 2 of *The Rainbow* Tom has to fight Anna for his place in her mother's bed, only taking her as his daughter when the mother is absent in childbirth, in a quietly intense scene when the pair, small sobbing child and a stepfather concerned to make her his, feed the cows together. But even here, as the child on his knee, wrapped in a shawl, briefly takes the place of her mother for her father, she also stands in for *his* mother, and repositions him as son:

> And the two sat still listening to the snuffing and breathing of cows feeding in the sheds communicating with this small barn. The lantern shed a soft, steady light from one wall. All outside was still in the rain. He looked down at the silky folds of the paisley shawl. It reminded him of his mother. She used to go to church in it. He was back again in the old irresponsibility and security, a boy at home. (*R.* 79)

This is an interesting reworking of Mrs Morel and Paul. The little girl has become mother, the father son. Later in *The Rainbow* a more conventional Oedipal connection repeats these images again, though, through Will Brangwen (little Anna's future husband) and *his* future daughter Ursula, the Oedipal love of *Sons and Lovers* reworked in service of a rather happier conclusion (Ursula's eventual independence). Mother Anna turns her attention to the baby Gudrun, leaving the small Ursula and her father Will to work through their daughter–father dynamic:

> So Ursula became the child of her father's heart. She was the little blossom, he was the sun. (*R.* 213)

> How he loved that little Ursula – his heart had been sharply seared for her when he was a youth, first married. (*R.* 214)

And for Ursula it is simply that 'Her father was the dawn wherein her consciousness woke up'(*R.* 221). By the writing of *The Rainbow* this love can be cast as a positive context for the subject's development. What went wrong for Paul goes right for Ursula, as she uses, in an almost classically Freudian way, the relationship with her father as springboard, not impediment, to her adult relationships with men.

But as Tom's experience of the shawl which turns daughter into mother shows, no one in Lawrence is ever *simply* a son, or *simply* a mother. Part of the tension of Lawrence's family life comes from the fact that at any moment mother might become lover, or father son. When Anna hears of her father Tom's death much later in the novel, her motherhood is supplanted by her daughterhood:

> Since she had married and become a mother, the girl she had been was forgotten. Now, the shock threatened to break in upon her and sweep away all her intervening life, make her as a girl of eighteen again, loving her father. (*R.* 250)

The Rainbow has most clearly been read as a linear family saga, with the second generation supplanting and succeeding the first, and the third the second. The Brangwens, we are told in the novel's first sentence, 'had lived for generations on the Marsh Farm'. This ends with Ursula's rejection of domestic dependence, and with her miscarrying the fourth generation in the final chapter. The rural contact ends with Will's family's move to town to join 'the elite of Beldover'. But what is opened up at moments like this agony of grief which Anna experiences is the possibility that history is not linear, and that the self's past is always present. Later, Ursula asks her grandmother, Lydia, about Lensky, her biological grandfather, and 'thinking, she became again Lensky's girl-bride' (*R.* 256). This is more than memory, or at the very least it rewrites memory's easy relation to the past. In this conception of the subject, past and present collapse into each other across a nebulous sense of time as history.

'THE CHASM OF MEMORY'

Lawrence is then suggesting a self which has access to past selves in the present, and which experiences the past as present, especially at moments of crisis. Yet at the same time he was also trying to do something quite different, in working towards writing a self which is utterly foreign to itself – which recognizes its 'unknowableness', its 'darkness', and which refuses its relation to its own family history. I want now to look a little more closely at this issue: how Lawrence writes about loss, and about gaps, about self-*mis*recognition, self-alienation. Lawrence can write a self which is multi-relational, which is simultaneously mother, lover, daughter, at the same time young and old, existing at a number of points across time and all at the same time. What happens in Lawrence when the subject *cannot* recognize its past self – when the past is lost and a gap is gouged at the heart of its history?

The most obvious way into this is to consider class change, as the shifting context within which the self itself shifts (born, like Lawrence, into one world, living as always something of a foreigner in another). The Brangwens move to the town (from where they hope to 'represent culture', settling in the bourgeois house of the managing classes, *R*. 421–2): Tom was a farmer, Will is a draftsman, his daughter – the first woman to gain economic independence – becomes a teacher and goes to university. Paul Morel becomes a clerk and an artist rather than follow his father down the pit. The gamekeeper seduces her ladyship. At its most extreme and literal, Irishwoman Kate Leslie marries a Mexican and becomes a goddess. Geographical transition is crucial too, not just because people physically move, but because they then have to find their way as foreigners – Alvina Houghton in *The Lost Girl* moves from the Potteries to Italy, Aaron moves from London to Florence, Richard and Harriet Somers in *Kangaroo* move from England to Australia, Lydia Lensky from Poland to Derbyshire. Each move rends its own kind of chasm in the subject.

The self as traveller and as unfixed appears across Lawrence's work. Movement is at the heart of his project. 'My God, how far was she projected from her childhood, how far was she still to go? In one lifetime one travelled through æons', reflects Ursula in *Women in Love* as she passes through Continental Europe on a train with Birkin:

> The great chasm of memory from her childhood in the intimate country surroundings of Cossethay and the Marsh Farm – she remembered the servant Tilly, who used to give her bread and butter sprinkled with brown sugar, in the old living-room where the grandfather clock had two pink roses in a basket painted above the figures on the face – and now when she was travelling into the unknown with Birkin, an utter stranger – was so great, that it seemed she had no identity, that the child she had been, playing in the Cossethay churchyard, was a little creature of history, not really herself. (*WL* 481–2)

Here then is a self in flux, a self divided across its own history and unsure of what it is, a self looking at its past as the stuff of myth. The discussion of homelessness which Lawrence opens up here rests on an analysis of the rare fragility of home itself. Home is lost and gone, it was perhaps never actually how you remember it, but even in differentiating oneself from it (Ursula the child is 'not really herself', Ursula the woman), one shows one's dependence upon it.

But Lawrence writes about stasis as much as he writes about movement. It may be that transition or change is exactly what caused him finally to value stillness and fixity so much, despite the overwhelming sense of change which permeates his work. Departure, and this inability to settle, are ongoing anxieties which might explain the sovereign goal of Lawrence's philosophy: arrival in peace, self-awareness, stasis – the mythical rainbow's end which none of his narratives ever reach. 'They say it is better to travel than to arrive', he writes in *Fantasia*, of 'the journey of love':

> It's not been my experience, at least.... to come at last to a nice place under the trees with your 'amiable spouse'... And then to pitch a camp, and cook your rabbit, and eat him: and to possess your own soul in silence and to feel all the clamour lapse. That is the best I know. (*FU* 137–8)

If this is home, it must be constructed from the props which surround one, and it can only be reached when one stops, like a kind of death. However desirable it may be as a personal goal, it is clearly not desirable as a narrative one. There is little to say about silence, about the lapsed clamour, or even about the cooked rabbit. Narratives, selves, relationships, as Lawrence fully recognized, must keep moving.

But movement brings a risk – that of misrecognizing, or losing, that which one has left. Clearly, sometimes for Lawrence's characters the problem isn't disconnection with the past, but too much past ever-present. After Siegmund's suicide, his wife Beatrice tries to avoid facing up to her part in his death, her role in their shared past:

> She was afraid to meet the accusation of the dead Siegmund, with the seared jury of memories. When the event summoned her to stand before the bench of her own soul's understanding, she fled, leaving the verdict upon herself eternally suspected (*T.* 217)

Here, the past is a brick wall preventing reconciliation with the present and any possibility of a future. Elsewhere – as with this disconnected self-strange Ursula in *Women in Love* – the old self has taken with it all traces. Hers is a form of active forgetting like that which Nietzsche discusses, when the past is cast off as a source of guilt and responsibility, and if viewed at all appears like a picture-show, seen from the distance of a separate self. But what kind of self *can* do this – see one's past as someone else's movie, or forget it altogether? Only the self which is and always has been entirely alone – only the self which has the final say over what it is and what it has been. This is true of no one. In Lawrence, any existence is always guaranteed, challenged, confirmed by others. If our self-experience is multiple, and multi-layered in time, in memory, it is also multi-subjective. Our experience is not *only* our own.

So looking *back* from Ursula's experience on the train to a moment in the earlier novel when she is still a small child, we find that this kind of novelistic time-travel, which the self outside-of-itself engenders, is already at work. Already in *The Rainbow,* Lawrence casts us forward to *this* moment in *Women in Love,* but from the point of view of Ursula's *father.* Will is of course not present when Ursula experiences this 'chasm of memory' in *Women in Love,* although he does figure briefly in the novel. But for the father in *The Rainbow,* the 'now' Ursula on-the-train is still the 'then' Ursula in-the-home, the little girl who is not entirely her own because she is always part of her father's experience:

> Once she fell as she came flying to him, he saw her pitch forward suddenly as she was running with her hands lifted to him; and when he picked her up, her mouth was bleeding. He could never bear to think of it, he always wanted to cry, even when he was an old man and she had become a stranger to him. (*R.* 214)

Ursula's past, and her self, is thus not entirely her own to lose, remember, forget or reject; it is partly Will's. Will 'has' that moment with his daughter, close enough to be unbearable, even when *The Rainbow* gives way to *Women in Love,* the novel of Ursula's 'strangeness'. Of course, Will is not a 'real person' whose experience slides across the two novels, even though as a character he appears in both of them. What I am saying is that in a sense the first novel here anticipates the second, that the past and the future are closer than our conventions of linear time might have us think, and there is a point at which the closeness of memory and the strangeness of distance meet. The self is not its own. Experience casts forward, caught up in a memory which is almost bodily, blurring the limits of what a self thinks of as her 'own', and challenging the notion that it must be bound by its own time.

THE LOST PAST: NOTTINGHAM ESSAYS

A grander, national loss is also being worked through in Lawrence's writing, and this is not a loss which can be redeemed, or brought back, through memory. It is a loss which is also Lawrence's own, and which causes him to slip into a rare, directly autobiographical mode. Writing the self, and writing the self as something which is constructed through memory, are often the same thing with Lawrence; the present is an effect of one's embedded experience in the social, the familial, the community past. How then does the self, as a construction of memory and its own past experiences, think about itself when that material past is lost?

Ursula's 'great chasm of memory' is one way of exploring this. Lawrence's loosely autobiographical work might be another. Perhaps all of Lawrence's work should properly be seen as a kind of fusion between the autobiographical, the philosophical and the fictive. Lawrence wrote no conventional autobiography, but it could be argued that the autobiographical is present across a number of different forms of his work. One example of the kind of personal-intellectual story-telling at which he excels is his last, long polemical essay, *Apocalypse*. Basically an investigation of twentieth-century religious malaise, this begins, if not with personal anecdote, then grounded in the experience of working-class chapel-going at the turn of the century. Lawrence himself refused to equate life events with the evasive quality of a life: three short autobiographical essays written late in life, 'Hymns in a Man's Life' (1928), 'Autobiographical Sketch' (1929), and 'Nottingham and the Mining Countryside' (1929) blur the boundaries between individuality, culture and landscape, and fix personal identity firmly in a mystical sense of social history. The latter piece begins like a classic first person narrative novel:

> I was born nearly forty-four years ago, in Eastwood, a mining village of some three hundred souls, about eight miles from Nottingham. (*P*1 133)

Rather than ticking its way through events to the present, this then becomes an essay about place, not self, a cultural history of landscape and industry, with a sense of how Lawrence fitted into that landscape, of the writer placed within it, only implicitly present. 'Autobiographical Sketch', most promisingly, offers a few basic biographical co-ordinates, but ends as a diatribe against middle-class passionlessness, and Lawrence's feeling of being adrift from class fixity. Always a writer in-between, in 'Nottingham' he says that he 'came into consciousness' in a 'queer jumble of the old England and the new' (*P*1 135). But the old England is gone almost as soon as he brings it to the page. Written in France in the late 1920s by a Lawrence who had long ceased to live in England, something is clearly being resurrected from a distance. If this is biography, it is national biography; if this is present encountering the past, it is a national past rather than a personal past which Lawrence really wants to address. This national past, bound to a certain kind of labour, has already been rendered mythical by loss:

> To me, as a child and a young man, it was still the old England of the forest and agricultural past; there were no motor-cars, the mines were, in a sense, an accident on the landscape, and Robin Hood and his merry men were not very far away. (*P*1 133)

> the life was a curious cross between industrialism and the old agricultural England of Shakespeare and Milton and Fielding and George Eliot. (*P*1 135)

Whatever comes into writing is already lost and gone. This is an elegy: 'The mill only ceased grinding the corn when I was a child' (*P*1 135). Even positive statements about the existence of things ('The windlass mines were still working when my father was a boy – and the shafts of some were still there, when I was a boy', (*P*1 133) are laced with the implication that these things are no more. Saying that it was there is also a way of saying that now it is gone. Absence is implicit in the substance of memory. The recapturing, the holding-on-to, which remembering and representing something brings, is always undermined by the sense that if it is recalled it is already lost:

> I remember the great rolls of coarse flannel and pit-cloth which stood in the corner of my grandfather's shop when I was a small boy, and the big, strange old sewing machine, like nothing else on earth, which sewed the massive pit-trousers. But when I was only a child the company discontinued supplying the men with pit-clothes. (*P*1 133–4)

Writing of the effect that changes in mining practice had on miners themselves, Lawrence addresses a more general predicament of writing memory: 'They did not know what they had lost till they had lost it' (*P*1 136). If the self comes into being inextricably bound to its community as home, what happens to it when that community is lost? These essays act out a kind of cultural grieving process, underlining the fact that it is not only individual subjects, but the fabric from which they are cut, which was lost when Lawrence's world changed.

The first four stanzas of a curious poem from 1928, 'Red-Herring', which Lawrence included in his *Pansies* collection, set out this loss and estrangement as predicated on a divided home, a changed industrial base and the disorientations of class change:

> My father was a working man
>   and a collier was he,
> at six in the morning they turned him down
>   and they turned him up for tea.
>
> My mother was a superior soul
>   a superior soul was she
> cut out to play a superior rôle
>   in the god-damn bourgeoisie
>
> We children were the in-betweens
>   little non-descripts were we,
> indoors we called each other *you*,
>   outside, it was *tha* and *thee*.
>
> But time has fled, our parents are dead
>   we've risen in the world all three;
> but still we are in-betweens, we tread
>   between the devil and the deep cold sea.
>
> (*Poems*, 490)

Domesticity, it seems, equips you only for a life of wandering, misplacement, mis-fitting. Neither mother nor father, inside nor out, here nor there, the poem's children do not control the world they inhabit. If desire is to flourish, it must learn the language of the in-between, it must learn 'you' as well as 'thee'. The presence and absences of home – home read as a domestic, psychic or a cultural state – shape Lawrentian desire into a powerful but thwarted thing, which strives to live, in-between. Yet Lawrence, writer of plenitude *par excellence*, does not like this writing of absence and nostalgia, and he strives to champion positivity again: energy not ennui, being forged from becoming, desire rooted in having rather than wanting.

3

The Fox, the Cat and the Rabbit: Gender and its differences

> I can only write what I feel pretty strongly about: and that, at present, is the relations between men and women. After all, it is *the* problem of today, the establishment of a new relation, of the readjustment of the old one, between men and women. (*L*1 546)

Lawrence famously wrote that the most important thing to write about was the relationship between the sexes. He also wrote both that we must strive to keep the sexes pure, and that the difference between them is essential:

> We are wrong when we say that there is no vital difference between the sexes. There is every difference. Every bit, every cell in a boy is male, every cell is female in a woman, and must remain so. Women can never feel or know as men do. And in the reverse, men can never feel and know, dynamically, as women do. (*FU* 102)

However, this difference is only maintained – it only 'remains so' in Lawrence – an act of solitary exertion on the part of the man, and a corresponding submission by the woman:

> You've got to know that you're a man, and being a man means you go on alone, ahead of woman, to break a way through the old world into the new. And you've got to be alone. (*FU* 192)

As Lawrence wrote in a letter to Katherine Mansfield in November 1918, in order for man to be able to 'go ahead absolutely in front of their women, without turning round to ask for permission or for approval from their women', the woman must first 'yield some sort of precedence to a man', they must 'follow as it were unquestioningly'. Female submission is high on Lawrence's behavioural agenda. Speaking of both horses and women in *Women in Love*, Birkin argues that 'the last, perhaps highest, love-impulse' is to 'resign your will to the higher being' (*WL* 202).

Lawrence was obsessed with the position of women, their role, their sexuality. His novels are often the stories of women, privileging their perspective as the main narrative focus. Alvina Houghton, Ursula Brangwen, Constance Chatterley, Kate Leslie, unquestionably dominate the novels in which they feature. Yet they articulate such varied possibilities for feminine subjectivity that it is hard sometimes to believe that the polemical writer of sexual philosophy which Lawrence becomes in his non-fiction is the same as the exploratory analyst of women's point of view in his fiction. Nevertheless, a strident image of the sexual 'norm' – keeping the sexes pure, maintaining male supremacy through exertion and struggle – was increasingly to figure as the central tenet of Lawrence's *overt* philosophizing from around the writing of this letter. Again, in *The Plumed Serpent*, Kate anticipates the 'supreme passivity' of sex with Cipriano:

> Ah! and what a mystery of prone submission, on her part, this huge erection would imply! Submission absolute, like the earth under the sky. Beneath an over-arching absolute. (*PS* 325)

And in *Studies in Classic American Literature* Lawrence advocates or foresees 'the dark erection of the images of sex-worship once more, and the newly-submissive women' before offering a version of 'woman's right to choose' which feminist readers have found particularly objectionable: 'When we have at last broken this insanity of mental-spiritual consciousness... the women *choose* to experience again the great submission' (*SCAL* 101). In his idealized state, the religiously led post-revolution Mexico of *The Plumed Serpent*, men and women find a place in a landscape rendered, as Alastair Niven points out, 'in harsh images of male sexuality: phallic cacti and sperm-like water',[1] a fitting backdrop for a religion in which women cover their faces and sit on the floor, 'But men must stand erect':

> around the low dark shrubs of the crouching women stood a forest of erect, upthrusting men, powerful and tense with inexplicable passion. (*PS* 353, 355)

Ideal sexual difference, it seems, is even inscribed in nature, and when women submit and men stand straight (as nature intended) they cannot help but emulate natural forms. To crouch, as a woman, is then to be 'natural', or so this discourse runs. But not all of Lawrence's women *do* crouch, nor do his men stand erect, and there the interesting conflict comes. Sexual consummation ought to be the moment at which Lawrence's grand oppositional structure becomes most clear. Crisis moments are, however, often the points at which these structures begin to break down.

This sexualization of all phenomena is extrapolated into a general philosophical principle. In *Study of Thomas Hardy* Lawrence writes that 'The male exists in doing, the female in being' (*P*1 481). In *Fantasia of the Unconscious*, a text within which Lawrence vehemently criticizes Freud for attributing a sexual motive to all human activity, he nevertheless writes, 'Action and utterance, which are male, are polarised against feeling, emotion, which are female' (*FU* 98). Not only, then, is sexual difference the crux of our identities, it underpins everything which is *not* us too. Reality is marked by a traditional binary structure of sexual difference. More radically, the implication here is also that anything which acts or utters, even if it is a woman, is masculinized by her action, whilst that which feels – even if it is a man – is feminized. Gender mutates, shifts, exchanges, as Lawrence's figures work and move against themselves.

FEMINISM'S LAWRENCE

It would be difficult now to take some of these passages seriously as a prescription for submission, or, in the words of Simone de Beauvoir's pathbreaking reading of Lawrence in *The Second Sex*, as blueprints for women's behaviour. Even in a climate of nineties backlash, when so-called 'postfeminist' women increasingly feel the need to preface their timorous objections with 'I'm not a feminist but...', the idea that literary advocacy of ultimate submission to male power could be viewed as a genuine threat requiring an articulate feminist response is bizarre. We are now entering a new phase of Lawrence criticism, which still can't help but focus on the centrality of gender in his work but which would address the sexual power of these passages in fresh ways. Yet older modes of analysis still prevail. Whilst acknowledging that the phase of Messianic Lawrence-worship is over, Keith Brown laments the more recent emergence of a Lawrence investigated by literary theory:

'Simply to send [students] back to the text, unaided and with their reactions confused by half a dozen as yet only half-assimilated literary theories is not enough'. Then, in an extraordinary move to reinstate Lawrence-the-transcendent, wiser than us all, Brown positions the Great Man beyond the sway of trendy contemporary thought. Lawrence, he writes,

> is not only 'post-Leavis'. He is also 'post' the so-called student revolution, with its shifts, partly permanent, in all our perceptions of paternalistic authority; post the sexual revolution and its aftermath; post the feminist (or what was known at the time as 'women's lib') explosion; post the revivals of more traditional radicalism, left and right...[2]

– and so he continues, listing a whole range of critical and political positions which Lawrence has ostensibly foreseen, refuted and gone beyond.

I want to open up a Lawrence who is not 'post' feminism, but within feminism. This is not the same as saying that he is a feminist writer. But it may be that even a virulently sexist figure has an agenda akin to feminism's, in that his project is to identify, and perhaps protect or police, the boundary between the sexes. Lawrence's central concerns are sexual-political; his key focus is the relationship between the sexes, and – as I will explore in the next chapter – sexual relationships. As Hilary Simpson has argued in *D. H. Lawrence and Feminism* (1982), gender infuses the whole of Lawrence's culture:

> For Lawrence, everything is sexed; it is the fundamental division. The Hardy Study is permeated with a sense of sex-designated opposites. Maleness comprises Knowledge, the Spirit, Motion, Love, the Hub, Doing, Separateness, Consciousness, Individuality, Timelessness, Thought and the religion of the Son; Femaleness is Nature, the Flesh, Stability, Law, the Axle, Being, Monism, Unconsciousness, Oneness, the Moment, Feeling, and the religion of the Father.[3]

Lawrence then is a writer of sexuality even when he is not writing *about* sexuality – a factor ignored by many feminist critics who prefer to read him as a sexual thinker only when sexuality is his subject matter. Simpson also shows that his writing took place in reaction to and largely influenced by the 'explosion' of the first wave of feminism, the suffrage movement, and work today cannot help but engage with more recent feminist response.

It is often said that feminist criticism of Lawrence began in 1969 with the publication of Millett's *Sexual Politics*, even though Simone de Beauvoir's reading preceded this by twenty-odd years, and provides Millett with many of her key forms of analysis. However, we might also consider the trial of *Lady Chatterley's Lover* in 1960 as the event which most publicly set the terms for the twists and turns of feminist critique which followed. As C. H. Rolph writes in the introduction to his invaluable narrative transcript of the trial itself, puritan disgust at the novel soon became outrage at its heroine, whose behaviour challenged codes of feminine propriety (her sexual quest results in fulfilment), marriage vows (she commits adultery) and obscenity law (the affair is explicitly wrought with liberal use of 'offensive' language):

> Just how much it was she [Lady Chatterley], and not D. H. Lawrence or Penguin Books, who was on trial will appear from the following pages. It was a fifteenth-century trial for adultery, Constance Chatterley was there in Court, the Scarlet Letter must somewhere be ready.[4]

The significance of the acquittal of Lawrence, his novel, and its heroine herself in late 1960 had a crucial impact on the subsequent history of print, ushering in a much more liberal publishing climate within which a much wider range of sexual material could be bought, sold and written. At the start of the second wave of feminism, this was also a significant moment for women.

Lawrence's posthumous role in this moment cannot be underestimated, whether as, in Carol Dix's (I think misguided) terms, writer of 'female characters who were finally to emerge as real people in the sixties and seventies',[5] or as, in Norman Mailer's (perhaps even more misguided) terms, the prototype gender-bender, 'a man who had the soul of a beautiful, imperious, and passionate woman, yet he was locked in the body of a middling male physique'.[6] Not only was this moment crucial for the reception of his work in 'high' cultural circles, he was also more popularly perceived as guru to a generation rethinking traditional family and sexual structures. Of course, as I pointed out earlier, Lawrence was deeply committed to commitment itself, to marriage as 'the clue to human life', and to sexual exploration within the context of faithful heterosexuality. Despite these conventional constraints, the sixties Lawrence was to some of his readers 'a prophet of sexual freedom'; as Sheila MacLeod puts it:

> Whether you were in favour of letting it all hang out or just some good wholesome fucking, Lawrence was your ally and your advocate. And it was all right to call it fucking because, if the act were not shameful, so neither was the word.[7]

However, having been acquitted by the jury in the Old Bailey, Lawrence then became the site of a dialogue of prosecution and defence in the academy and on the page. I have argued elsewhere[8] that the terms of this discussion over gender and power came not just from the courtroom of 1960, but from Lawrence's own writing, since he was rather partial to using a little prosecuting rhetoric himself on the issue of undesirable sexual behaviour, role reversal and powerful women. In response we need a mode of feminist address which would read the text not in the language of a 'literary lawyer' (who, for Mailer, 'cannot do criticism, they can only write briefs'[9]), but as a contradictory work which cannot help but break its own codes and rules of behaviour.

It is important to acknowledge the stark and undeniable case which feminism in the seventies and eighties made against Lawrence. Just as it is impossible to read the history of British censorship this century without discussion of the *Lady Chatterley* trial, and of Lady Chatterley herself, so it is impossible to address Lawrence studies without reference to gender analysis. Through this knot of representation, the public life of texts, the legality and challenge of the image both written and visual, femininity is threaded. However, more recent developments have allowed us to turn back to gender issues in Lawrence's work and find a more complex interrelationship between the sexes which problematizes even as it desperately tries to maintain this rigid sexual division of identity and pleasure. Even those texts which seem to state Lawrence's gender agenda most extremely show that his much-vaunted 'vital difference between the sexes' is not as simple as it seems. The identity crisis at the heart of the sexual subject pervades even his most polemical writing on gender.

DIFFERENCE IN *THE FOX*

Lawrence's short novel of 1918, *The Fox*, has often been taken as proof positive that his discourse of unconscious bodily knowledge is itself embedded in misogyny. Kate Millett's analysis of the story in *Sexual Politics* pioneered this approach, reading its male character as its main point of sympathy or identification, and its female characters as the focus of vilification or narrative contempt. Certainly *The Fox* articulates a battle, perhaps the clearest battle of the sexes in Lawrence's corpus. Two women live together in an unlucky and unnatural life of inexplicit lesbianism, raising hens who are prey to the local fox, struggling against a natural order from which they are entirely alienated. One (March) is masculinized by the arrangement, whilst the other (Banford) dwindles into a fretful, manipulative caricature of passive-aggressive femininity. A stranger – a soldier returned from the Great War – intrudes, moves in, shoots the fox which has become the sign of natural masculinity outwitting the embattled and abnormal women, dispatches Banford, his rival for the love of March, by felling a tree onto her, and so wins the hand of March. March is womanized in the process. For Kate Millett, killing Banford also kills March, who submits to a 'drugged loss of self'.[10]

Reading the story with a wider range of interdisciplinary tools, we might equally focus on how power is manifested here through the twists of visual dominance between male and female characters, by eliciting theories of the male gaze which have burgeoned within film and media studies. This would identify the oppressive effect of the male look as agent of the visual objectification of the women in *The Fox*. The clearest example of this is the incessant visual aggression of Henry, the soldier who kills Banford. However, even before he appears, March has an encounter with the fox which prefigures her relations with Henry himself. For all of Lawrence's adamance that nature is *other* – even in this story – he readily slides into anthropomorphism, as the fox itself becomes bearer of an explicit 'male gaze' which obliterates her individual agency:

> She lowered her eyes, and suddenly saw the fox. He was looking up at her. Her chin was pressed down, and his eyes were looking up.

> They met her eyes. And he knew her. She was spellbound – she knew he knew her. So he looked into her eyes, and her soul failed her. He knew her, he was not daunted.... he had lifted his eyes upon her, and his knowing look seemed to have entered her brain. She did not so much think of him: she was possessed by him. ... She felt him invisibly master her spirit. (*CSN* 138–9)

This absurd encounter, in which fox outmans woman by virtue of his overarching masculine prowess, sets the pattern for the gender conflicts which unfold when Henry arrives. There is no way that Lawrence's fox could be a vixen. Masculinity brings visual consciousness to the household, as Lawrence details again and again in passages beginning 'The youth watched her' or 'his eyes came back to her' (*CSN* 144, 145). The women, newly awakened to the experience of appearance, shrink into acute self-consciousness – falling under his 'steady, penetrating looks' March 'was almost ready to disappear' (*CSN* 145). The sexual battle here thus takes place explicitly within a visual agenda within which men look and women are seen. The male gaze penetrates, and its female object tries and fails to escape into invisibility, just like the hens. For looking here finally means killing; to be seen is to be prey:

> He would have to catch her as you catch a deer or a woodcock when you go out shooting. It's no good walking out into the forest and saying to the deer: 'Please fall to my gun.' No, it is a slow, subtle battle. (*CSN* 153)

Read in the frame of Lawrence's wider visual theories, this balance of power is surprising. Elsewhere – indeed as I have argued in *Sex in the Head, everywhere* else in Lawrence – visual prowess is entirely aligned with a degenerate, all-too-cerebral femininity gripped by the desire to know through the look, to have, possess, sadistically control through visual consciousness. That Lawrence also – contrarily – painted, wrote plays (visual dramas), and presented scenes of homoerotic visual pleasure (spectacles of men enjoyed through the disavowed and condemned eyes of his female narrative points of view), subverts but does not erase this primary 'message', that modern culture's fetishization of visual pleasure underpins its sickness.

Thus it is strange to find a male figure so committed to looking, and a female opposition so helpless in the face of it, within a story which seems to be such an anthem to masculine primitivism defeating feminine wilfulness. A few moments of familiar masculine alignment with the 'darkness' do remain in the story, although here 'invisibility' does the same work: 'even before you come in sight of your quarry', Henry thinks to himself, 'there is a strange battle, like mesmerism.... It is a subtle, profound battle of wills which takes place in the invisible' (*CSN* 104). Yet it is women here who are most at home 'in the invisible', women who, indeed, find it hard to look at all ('It made [Banford] feel a little ill to look at him' *CSN* 158), and find it even harder to be seen.

This much might confirm Millett's position on the story. Henry looks, dominates, kills: the fox is shot in an act which allows male-human to absorb its male-animal power. Banford is murdered, March is subdued into a submissive state which is tantamount to rigor mortis. But however much Henry's active dominance is finally privileged, the narrative frame of *The Fox* actually remains the experience of the women. Henry is the catalyst, an agent of change, a stranger, an intruder, but his action takes place within the context of the women's landscape, a psychological and material landscape they have fashioned and which precedes his arrival. Whilst Banford does not survive till the story's end, and the last words are indeed Henry's, March does not entirely accede to him. Her ultimate prevarication, her refusal and ambivalence, means that *The Fox*, like many of Lawrence's tales and novels, ends without an ending, closes with no sense of closure. The sexual story remains open by virtue of woman's refusal finally to submit.

MASTERY AND INEQUALITY

Clearly there is something deeply misogynistic about the way in which *The Fox* deals its sexual hand, particularly the contempt with which the sorry Banford is represented and dispatched. Yet clearest of all is the picture it presents of sexual life as a battle, of the sex war waged on every level of everyday life from breakfast to bedtime and through into our dreams. Like the most ardent of feminist campaigners, Lawrence – probably from the other side of the barricades – plots the points of conflict meticulously, asks that we do not muddy the waters of sexual violence with sympathy and sentimentality for the enemy or ourselves, sets out a fundamental opposition between men and women and requires his characters to conform to it. 'Very good, she was the enemy, very good', exults Anna in *The Rainbow* during a conflict with Will, her husband: 'As he prowled round her, she watched him. As he struck her, she struck back' (*R.* 63). Both Lawrence and feminism are well aware that stories narrate our cultural understandings back to us and give us a frame for our development as subjects. For both, sexuality infuses all personal and public acts; for both, sexual division is central to the organization of social reality. The personal is the political was the famous refrain of seventies feminism. In his writing, Lawrence renders all personal response innately political because the personal is sexual and the sexual is political. We need to think about Lawrence's obsession with the relationship between the sexes as itself part of a wider ongoing discussion about inequality.

Seldom are Lawrence's men and women at peace. 'Equilibrium' is a word he is far more likely to use than 'peace', an equilibrium which recognizes difference but values balance. A common image for the ideal relationship is that of two stars suspended and orbiting each other, balanced in separation but absolutely bound to each other's movements. Equality is a trickier term, since it is precisely *in*equality and its tensions which is so often explored and relished here. 'There is no such thing as equality', he proclaims in 'Reflections on the Death of a Porcupine' (*P2* 473). In 'The Spirit of Place', he sets up his lengthy critique of the diseased American psyche as based on democracy. Americans see themselves as a masterless race, 'A vast republic of escaped slaves' (*SCAL* 11). But since finally, for Lawrence, 'men cannot live without masters', they constructed Old Europe as the still-present, absent master, the image to oppose as well as to obey with a 'slow, smouldering, corrosive obedience' (*SCAL* 10–11). Disease results; emasculation – the American Eagle is 'a Hen-Eagle'. The message: know your place, know your enemy, affirm openly your position in the roll-call of mastery.

This may sound like authoritarianism, a totalitarian assertion of social and biological fixity. What does emerge from this is a clear challenge, a call for the battle-lines to be drawn. This is conflict theory at its extreme. I mentioned earlier how 'Reflections on the Death of a Porcupine' develops an idiosyncratic evolutionary theory which positions the dandelion higher than the fern in terms of *'vive'* (life) appeal, but Lawrence does not stop there. He outlines a whole natural order stratified according to relationships of mastery. To be 'vividly alive' is to be in a position to master something: 'If the lower cycles of life are not *mastered*, there can by no higher cycle', he writes (*P*2 467). For Lawrence, the key issue of 'vival' as well as 'survival' prompts the question of whether life is built on dominance. *'Can thy neighbour finally overcome thee?'* he asks (*P*2 468). 'Life' or liveliness is determined by the answer – upon a yes or a no, Lawrence's natural-social system is built:

> Life is more vivid in the snake than in a butterfly.
> Life is more vivid in a wren than in an alligator.
> Life is more vivid in a cat than in an ostrich.
> Life is more vivid in the Mexican who drives the wagon, than in the two horses in the wagon.
> Life is more vivid in me, than in the Mexican who drives the wagon for me.
>
> (*P*2 468)

He qualifies this, of course, urging that we nevertheless view each single individual being on its own terms, and cease to compare unlike with unlike. Never one to pass up the opportunity to contradict himself, Lawrence also writes on the question of himself qua Mexicans in *Studies*: 'When I meet another man, and he is just himself – even if he is an ignorant Mexican pitted with smallpox – then there is no question between us of superiority or inferiority. He is a man and I am a man' (*SCAL* 50). However, the racial gist of the 'Porcupine' comparison is apparently justified because the master race, for the brief time it masters, accesses the power which bestows vitality – 'One race of man can subjugate and rule another race' he writes here, but in *The Plumed Serpent* and 'The Woman Who Rode Away' he was to explore what would happen when that 'mastery' passes from one race to another, from – as he puts it – the blue eyes back to the brown.

So far there is nothing here about gender difference, but we do not have to look much further. In a moment I will look at an episode in *Women in Love*, when Mino the tom-cat subdues a female stray by simple assertion of the mastery Lawrence sketches out in the 'Porcupine' essay. Sexual struggles between female victim and male aggressor break out across Lawrence's work, in fantasy, in perception, and acted out. After Lawrence has positioned the Mexican below him, he positions the woman below him too. In *The Plumed Serpent* woman is full of resentment at her lot, imbued with an 'inevitable mistrust and lurking insolence, insolent against a higher creation'. Her spirit of protest is likened to 'the striking of a snake' (*PS* 84). Woman is 'below' because she is 'taken', she is mastered. Sex is not just consummation, but consuming – a consuming which enables the absorber to rise above the absorbed, to transcend her by feeding on her. 'The primary way... to get vitality', he writes again in 'Death of a Porcupine', 'is to absorb it from living creatures lower than ourselves': 'There are many ways of absorbing: devouring food is one way, love is often another' (*P2* 469). Man devours, woman is devoured. This is what happens when she 'yields precedence'.

'There is no equality' – certainly not in sexual relationships. This unequal power relation is something which Lawrence returns to across his writing. But despite what he says about the subordination of women in his essays (which might be cast more as wish-fulfilment than truth-telling), it is not always the case in the fiction. Early in *The Rainbow* Will certainly 'takes' Anna like predator pouncing on prey:

> He came to her fierce and hard, like a hawk striking and taking her. He was not mystic any more, she was his aim and object, his prey. And she was hurried off, and he was satisfied, or satiated at last. (*R.* 162–3)

The use of the verb 'take' to mean 'fuck' in Lawrence incorporates this whole understanding of sex as power, sex as incorporation, as bodily taking-in. But here sexual relations do not conform to a straightforward gender agenda. Women give as good as they get, and if they aren't actively turning on men in an attempt to take on the mantle of mastery themselves, they are using the victim's position as their paradoxical seat of inverted power. Reading on, Anna turns the tables by deploying her victimage as a weapon. Extending this bird imagery until it capitulates, until the sides switch and active becomes passive, victim becomes violator, Anna 'the pathetic plover' uses her subordination as a mask of cover:

> She too was a hawk. If she imitated the pathetic plover running plaintive to him, that was part of the game.... her soul roused, its pinions became like steel, and she struck at him. When he sat on his perch glancing sharply round with solitary pride, pride eminent and fierce, she dashed at him and threw him from his station savagely, she goaded him from his keen dignity of a male... till he was mad with rage, his light brown eyes burned with fury.... like flames of anger they flared at her and recognised her as the enemy. (*R.* 163)

This is a sexual game not unlike that which is to develop between Gerald Crich and Anna's second daughter, Gudrun, in *Women in Love,* in which the sadistic Gudrun is certainly ultimately dominant. However, at first Gerald too is a hawk. On meeting the model Pussum in the bohemian Pompadour café in the same novel, Gerald's attraction is

> an instinctive cherishing very near to cruelty. For she was a victim. He felt that she was in his power, and he was generous. The electricity was turgid and voluptuously rich in his limbs. He would be able to destroy her utterly in the strength of his discharge. (*WL* 117)

But is Pussum a victim because she is a woman, and is her femininity a necessary component of her victimage? Norman Mailer wrote of Lawrence,

> Never had a male novelist written more intimately about women – heart, contradiction, and soul; never had a novelist loved them more, been so comfortable in the tides of their sentiment, and so ready to see them murdered.[11]

Lawrence jumbles his terms across his work, and not all, or perhaps not even *most* of his victims are female. Men, too, are dispatched, in body and in fantasy, and the spectacle of their sexualized deaths is both exquisite and unique. Later in *The Rainbow* it is Ursula, Anna's first-born, who, vampire-like, feeds off Skrebensky. The struggle for control which animates this pair's every sexual meeting is almost the dramatization of Lawrence's 'Porcupine' argument about mastery attained through consumption, but with the mistress as master. Skrebensky loses the battle:

> His will was set and straining with all its tension to encompass him

> and compel her. If he could only compel her. He seemed to be annihilated. (*R.* 320)

Kisses are the channel through which Ursula confirms her control. The mouth thus becomes the opening which unites those two forms of absorption which Lawrence mentions in 'Porcupine', eating and loving. This kiss allows Ursula to 'take' Skrebensky, twice over:

> Even, in his frenzy, he sought for her mouth with his mouth, though it was like putting his face into some awful death.... Till gradually his warm, soft iron yielded, yielded, and she was there fierce, corrosive, seething with his destruction, seething like some cruel, corrosive salt around the last substance of his being, destroying him, destroying him in the kiss. And her soul crystallized with triumph, and his soul was dissolved with agony and annihilation. (*R.* 321-2)

What is interesting here is not just that this is almost text-book sado-masochism, nor that it is the woman who is victor. It is that in the midst of this frenzy Lawrence, for all his proclamations about man as master, chooses to identify with, and to articulate this from the position of the loser, the victim, the absorbed. Who is doing what to whom, and which position is finally preferable, is not as clear as it would seem. Complicity in sexual exchange is central. In *Women in Love* Birkin reflects that 'It takes two to make a murder – a murderer and a murderee', whilst in 'The Escaped Cock' Lawrence sees Christ's impulse to save as absolutely bound up with Mary Madeleine's desire to be saved. And in the early poem 'Love on the Farm' (*Poems*, 42–3), written from the victim's point of view which is also the woman's point of view, the desires of doer and done-to are perfectly matched. First she imagines the approaching man's previous act of mastery, her terror building up as he returns to deal with her as he has dealt with the (female) rabbit he has just killed:

> ...then with wild spring
> Spurts from the terror of his oncoming;
> To be choked back, the wire ring
> Her frantic effort throttling:
>   Piteous brown ball of quivering fears!
> Ah, soon in his large, hard hands she dies,
> And swings all loose from the swing of his walk!

These stages in the murder – taking, domination and eventually consumption – are all repeated in the second part of the poem, when the man comes to the woman:

> I hear his hand on the latch, and rise from my chair,
> Watching the door open; he flashes bare
> His strong teeth in a smile, and flashes his eyes
> In a smile like triumph upon me; then careless-wise
> He flings the rabbit soft on the table board
> And comes towards me: ah! the uplifted sword
> Of his hand against my bosom! and oh, the broad
> Blade of his glance that asks me to applaud
> His coming! With his hand he turns my face to him
> And caresses me with his fingers that still smell grim
> Of the rabbit's fur!

The climax – the speaker's 'death' – is ecstatic. She slips into a darkness bestowed by the killer's look, his mouth – like Ursula's – 'hooding' her consciousness like the hood of the executed, like the wire around the rabbit's neck:

> And down his mouth comes to my mouth! and down
> His bright dark eyes come over me, like a hood
> Upon my mind! his lips meet mine, and a flood
> Of sweet fire sweeps across me, so I drown
> Against him, die, and find death good.

Which is most delicious? Submission to this Sadeian, bodice-ripping, Regency Rake, or the experience of mastery itself? Am I the doer or the done to, in reading this? Am I hunter or hunted? The answer is anything but clear. Lawrence wants both – submission and domination, all in one. We cannot help but wonder just what is at stake in his incessant fantasies which position us, and him, *with* the woman experiencing the beauty of the male, murderous, masterful or not. I will return to this in the last section of this chapter, when I come to look at what passes between men.

SUBMISSION (OR NOT): *THE FOX* (AGAIN)

But what are the implications of all this for the apparently stark clarity which pervades the savage sexual division and conflict of *The Fox*? Is March annihilated? Having absorbed the fox's authority, does Henry take March as Ursula took Skrebensky?

We might start again by invoking that opening quote from *Fantasia of the Unconscious*: 'Every bit, every cell in a boy is male, every cell is female in a woman, and must remain so'. March has foolishly tried to close the gap, erase the difference, take the man's part. The vehemence of the battle Lawrence stages in *The Fox* can then partly be attributed to his wider contempt for the sexual blurring of modernity's decadence, for it was the flapper and the fop and the dandy who most urgently suggested that girls will be boys and boys will be girls, well before more recent postmodern gender-bending. Henry's aim seems finally to be nothing more nor less than to establish a pure distinction of the sexes, a re-establishment of that natural mastery Lawrence is so unsure about elsewhere in his work:

> Then he would have all his own life as a young man and a male, and she would have all her own life as a woman and a female. There would be no more of this awful straining. She would not be a man any more, an independent woman with a man's responsibility. (*CSN* 205)

I want to pause briefly on that repeated word 'would'. A Millettian reading might focus on the wilfulness and determination of the word – the inevitability of this rigid sexual distinction coming to pass, the authoritarian assertiveness of Henry's desire. I would prefer to emphasize the singular unfinished quality of this extraordinarily inconclusive conclusion. Henry speaks a desire which remains incessantly unfulfilled, a *projection* of a desire, not its triumph or actualization. Nothing of this sexual divisiveness has come to pass by the time the story concludes, nor does the story promise or guarantee that it actually will. The passage echoes, and can be contrasted with, March's own thoughts a page or so earlier, in which Lawrence emphasizes the woman's wilfulness through italicizing the repeated 'would'. Again, degenerate femininity is aligned with struggling consciousness, and submission to a rightful and authentic femininity mastered by the man is likened to submission to sleep. March struggles to keep awake:

> She *would* keep awake. She *would* know. She *would* consider and judge and decide. She *would* have the reins of her own life between her own hands. She *would* be an independent woman to the last. But she was so tired, so tired of everything. (*CSN* 204)

This emphatic feminine '*would*' holds out till the story's

conclusion, a determined linguistic sign of March's wilful refusal ultimately to submit. *Her 'would'* is then the element which finally ensures that *his* 'would' means something different. If the woman '*would* consider and judge and decide' – as she always has done – then the man, stripped of the emphatic force of italics, is left only with a *wishful* 'would', a 'would' which speaks not self-certainty and control but desire for the as-yet-unfulfilled. Of course, as with the conclusion to 'The Woman Who Rode Away' (which I will look at in chapter 4), the tide of the narrative strongly implies that the man's 'would' will indeed come to pass, even though the story does not show us this. The metaphor of correct genderization in *The Fox* is falling asleep, a natural inevitability which will result once March has been sufficiently worn down (in this sense the story is curiously like Don Siegel's 1956 sci-fi classic film *Invasion of the Body Snatchers*, when sleep becomes the element within which the insidious conformity of the aliens is achieved). Yet we move towards the final full stop and still March is 'awake', her own self and not his, holding on as the story's sexual sticking point. Responding to his reassurance that she will feel 'better' when they emigrate, she says, ambivalently,

> 'Yes, I may. I can't tell. I can't tell what it will be like over there.'

Although Henry then has the final word ('"If only we could go soon!" he said, with pain in his voice'), this whole undecidable ending, which closes nothing, must be set alongside those other narrative prevarications, the endings of *Women in Love, The Plumed Serpent, Sons and Lovers, Lady Chatterley's Lover*, all of which conclude with more questions than answers, often with femininity, distance, sexual dissonance and confusion acting as the point of refusal, the element which prevents closure. What men and women are is never achieved, never finished. Who controls, who masters, remains the undecidable site of strife.

THE PASSION TO BE MASCULINE: *WOMEN IN LOVE*

The interchange of domination and submission laid out above is worked through in a number of ways in the sexual relationships of *Aaron's Rod, The Plumed Serpent, John Thomas and Lady Jane,*

Kangaroo, The Lost Girl. However, these are also not texts which *simplistically* foreground the merits of 'the great submission', and the homoeroticism of some of these tales muddies the waters further. More interesting than misogynistic assertions of patriarchal rights is the way in which Lawrence breaks his own rules, decidedly failing to 'know he's a man', and entering into 'the great submission' from the *wrong* side of the gender-tracks. In the next chapter I will think about what pleasure is in Lawrence, and what its relationship to dominance is: how the clearly advocated fulfilment which comes when the ego (particularly the female ego) submits to phallic assertion sometimes gives way to other more *nefarious* forms of gratification which challenge Lawrence's sense of heterosexual propriety, so that enjoyment of the forbidden, an indulgence in that which the text has forbidden itself, becomes possible, and identifying across the gender lines becomes necessary.

But it is only recently that Lawrence's fascination with and commitment to masculinity has begun to be investigated as thoroughly as were his representations of women in the seventies and eighties. If Lawrence castigated women, he also idolized men like few other modern writers, and this is not to contradict my earlier discussion of those images of masculine crisis in his work – the excluded father, the mother-fixated son, the unfulfilled lover. Against these must be set the ideal images which briefly emerge: crisis must be seen as a measure of failure, as the crumbling of a standard or ideal which is also fleetingly present. Norman Mailer's eulogy to Lawrence (and critique of Millett) in *The Prisoner of Sex* opens up the sexual contradiction at the heart of Lawrence's work (and reminds us once again of how hard it is to separate biography and fiction):

> [Lawrence] illuminates the passion to be masculine as no other writer, he reminds us of the beauty of desiring to be a man, for he was not much of a man himself, a son despised by his father, beloved of his mother, a boy and young man and prematurely ageing writer with the soul of a beautiful woman.[12]

Women in Love is perhaps Lawrence's most extended exploration of the potential of men-only relationships. As sequel to *The Rainbow*, its initial focus is the earlier novel's central character Ursula, and her sister Gudrun, both teachers who still live in the family home. Across the course of the novel the sisters form sexual relationships with Rupert Birkin, a school inspector who breaks his long-standing relationship with the aristocratic Hermione Roddice to marry Ursula, and Gerald Crich, a local mine-owner, who employs Gudrun to teach art to his sister, before entering into a savage sexual liaison with her, which culminates in Gerald's suicide. The action moves from the working-class Midlands to the bohemian country house, to avant-garde London and then on to mainland Europe, for the final tragic episode in the snow-bound Tyrol. It is undoubtedly Lawrence's most intellectually ambitious work, threading complex debates about sexuality and human identity, the importance of art, modernism, the war and Europe, in and out and through the interrelationships of its four protagonists. I want to look briefly at just one of these issues, concerning changing masculinity and the conditions of love between men.

In an infamous scene in chapter 13, as Birkin and Ursula debate the nature of their relationship, a scrap breaks out between Birkin's tom-cat, Mino, and a visiting female. Mino establishes his ostensibly innate dominance, convincing the female of the quality of his masculinity by cuffing her about a bit. Lawrence choreographs the cat-fight more like a ballet than a boxing-match, and Birkin eggs on the tom. It is left to Ursula to protest against Mino's behaviour: 'You are a bully like all males', she says to the unheeding animal. But Birkin defends his brother-in-gender (their complicity sealed by the glance which passes between man and cat 'in distain of the noisy woman'), urging Mino to 'Keep [his] male dignity, and [his] higher understanding', and explaining to Ursula,

> with the Mino, it is the desire to bring this female cat into a pure stable equilibrium, a transcendent and abiding rapport with the single male. Whereas without him, as you see, she is a mere stray, a fluffy bit of chaos. (*WL* 213)

Masculinity is thus in part the instrument of female-taming; its goal is to render woman the 'satellite' of man, to continue the terms of Birkin and Ursula's debate. But it seldom achieves this. The scene closes with Birkin and Ursula agreeing to differ, preferring to eat tea instead. Yet the assertion of masculinity in Lawrence is so often part of a primal gender struggle that it seems femininity must always be implicated in its definition. But men do not always win. Like the cock dominating his harem of hens, believing utterly in his 'higher understanding' despite the string which ties him down, his province is limited, his power finally challenged.

But men do not exist in Lawrence solely in relation to women. What, then, do Lawrence's men mean to each other? Tom-cat and queen may emblematically stand in for Birkin and Ursula, struggling for dominance, but the terms shift when Birkin and Gerald meet. Well over a decade before Virginia Woolf lamented the absence of novelistic story-lines which sketched out simply that 'Chloe liked Olivia', Lawrence wrote 'Gerald really loved Birkin'. In the 1929 essay 'The State of Funk', Lawrence writes, 'it is this that I want to restore into life: just the natural warm flow of common sympathy between man and man, man and woman' (*P2* 569). One route through to the first part of this is the blood-brotherhood proposed by Birkin between himself and Gerald, in answer to 'the problem of love and eternal conjunction between two men' (*WL* 277). Quite what 'loving Gerald all along, and all along denying it' means is never made entirely clear – if Birkin wants and disavows a fully homosexual connection, Lawrence equally explores and then disavows ('all along denying it') homoerotic elements in his work. It may be that he prefers to allow all types of relationships to exist between people of either sex, and that his suspicion of the strictly homosexual is a suspicion of categories. It may be that Lawrence strives towards a more open polymorphous connection between people; the different kinds of love which Birkin strives for.

So what – to rephrase Freud's famous phrase – do Lawrence's men want? Birkin wants the two of them to 'swear to stand by each other – be true to each other – ultimately – infallibly – giving to each other, organically – without the possibility of taking back' (*WL* 278). The men struggle to articulate what this might mean throughout the novel, even beyond Gerald's death. Birkin strives to raise the understanding of his love in Gerald's mind to the level of Gerald's love for Gudrun: 'I've loved you, as well as Gudrun, don't forget', he says as the two men part for the last time. But much of what passes between men resonates through descriptions of their bodies. In a novel where people behave with such astonishing articulacy, it is not so much what they say as how they touch which defines male space:

> Gerald came near the bed and stood looking down at Birkin whose throat was exposed, whose tossed hair fell attractively on the warm brow, above the eyes that were so unchallenged and still in the satirical face. Gerald, full-limbed and turgid with energy, stood unwilling to go, he was held by the presence of the other man. (*WL* 281)

The scene is not unlike that exemplary moment in *Aaron's Rod*, much quoted in evidence of Lawrence's homosexuality, when Aaron, also ill, prone, submissive, is ministered to by the stronger Lilly. In fact it might be said that the whole of *Aaron's Rod* is a debate about post-World War I masculinity and its discontents, especially the role of man inside or outside of the family: 'marriage wants readjusting', says Lilly, 'to get men on to their own legs once more, and to give them the adventure again' (*AR* 124). But what passes between men and women is not the context here for what passes between men and men. Women are entirely absent from the scene in which Lilly rubs the sick Aaron's body with oil. Although the passage is prefaced with a nurturing justification from Lilly ('I am going to rub you as mothers do their babies whose bowels don't work'), this is more than a substitute femininity, more than a men-only maternalism which countermands the abjection of female mothering we saw in chapter 2. It is male bodily contact which, if not sexual, passes through all the stages of sexual arousal, climax and exhaustion, building from a 'slow, rhythmic, circulating motion, a sort of massage', rubbing 'over the whole of the lower body, mindless, as if in a sort of incantation', speeding up, then relaxing into exhaustion (*AR* 118).

The scene is exemplary, not only for its closet homoeroticism, but also for its silent physicality. For all the impossible articulacy of the voices of *Women in Love*, the most valued moments between men happen between their bodies – if not in direct touch then in the exchange of gestures, glances, observations and admiration. In fact most of the physical contact between Lawrence's men is positive or nurturing: seldom do they fight, and if they do, this is one stage towards fuller understanding (think of Paul Morel and Baxter Dawes). Violence is far more likely to break out between men and women. In chapter 20 of

Women in Love Birkin and Gerald wrestle as the consolidation of their blood-brotherhood, in a scene which resonates with consummate male desire:

> So the two men entwined and wrestled with each other, working nearer and nearer.... It was as if Birkin's whole physical intelligence interpenetrated into Gerald's body, as if his fine, sublimated energy entered into the flesh of the fuller man (*WL* 348–9)

Prophet of heterosexuality Lawrence might be, but he also struggles to find a language – perhaps a homosexual language embedded within his heterosexuality – to name male beauty. And so the scene goes on, with the two men penetrating and withdrawing, writhing and gasping, making a literal beast with two backs even if Lawrence would finally have it that this is not sex, but may be beyond it:

> Often, in the white interlaced knot of violent living being that swayed silently, there was no head to be seen, only the swift, tight limbs, the solid white backs, the physical junction of two bodies clenched into oneness. (*WL* 349)

And so when Gerald dies as the result of his failures with a woman, Birkin regrets that their brotherhood had not been strong enough to save him, and is left unfulfilled, restless, wanting but denied the two kinds of love he tries to articulate. Masculinity is finally suspended and divided by its own contradictory desires, dependent on what it wants, what it cannot control. In the next chapter I will look at this again, exploring how Lawrence's notorious battles for dominance, played out through the heterosexual sex-act, are his key scenes of excitement and failure, with the struggle for precedence becoming the crucible of a contradictory modern identity.

4

Dangerous Pleasures and Dark Sex

> Love is the mysterious vital attraction which draws things together, closer, closer together. For this reason sex is the actual crisis of love. For in sex the two blood-systems, in the male and female, concentrate and come into contact, the merest film intervening. Yet if the intervening film breaks down, it is death. (*SCAL* 71)

> The only thing to do is to get your bodies back, men and women. ('Men Must Work and Women As Well', *P2* 591)

Much has been written about sex as gender, and about sexuality, in Lawrence, but what about sex itself? A commitment to consummate sexual experience is the central element of Lawrence's writing and philosophy. In 'The Real Thing', his 1927 diatribe against the women's movement, he writes,

> Love between man and woman is neither worship nor adoration, but something much deeper, much less showy and gaudy, part of the very breath, and as ordinary, if we may say so, as breathing. (*P1* 199)

Full sexuality is, however, dependent upon the achieved individual sexual identities of the two players as man and woman. As I argued in chapter 3, feminist cultural critique partly cut its teeth on readings of Lawrence as exemplary literary misogynist. This has meant that all subsequent analysis of Lawrence, even vehemently anti-feminist or ostensibly apolitical readings, must engage in some sort of defensive evasion of the early feminist case. However, more recent psychoanalytically informed analyses, or work drawing upon gay theory, have argued for a much more sexually contradictory Lawrence than this rather monolithic masculine monster. Rather than oppose with a countervailing critique, we might instead read Lawrence against himself. There is a desperation in his polemicizing, in his insistent assertion of the strictures of roles.

All of his work can be read as an anxious investigation of how the messiness of existence fails to fit into a neatly organized system of binary qualities, however hard Lawrence at times might want to make the system stick. I began chapter 3 with a quote from *Fantasia of the Unconscious* on the difference of men and women. Lawrence continues a little later:

> The whole mode, the whole everything is really different in man and woman. Therefore we should keep boys and girls apart, that they are pure and virgin in themselves. On mixing with one another, in becoming familiar, in being 'pals', they lose their own male and female integrity. And they lost the treasure of the future, the vital sex polarity, the dynamic magic of life. For the magic and the dynamism rests on *otherness*. (*FU* 103)

Readings of Lawrence's sexism focus on the way in which he characterizes these differences according to a traditional polarity, so that feminity is identified with emotion, masculinity with thought and purpose. Whilst I do not think that these qualities are irrelevant (they do, after all, underpin Lawrence's misogyny), feminist readings have focused on the limitations and unfairness of this gender stereotyping, the political and social denigration of the qualities ascribed to women, the traditional potency of those aligned with maleness. The main argument Lawrence is making here, however, lies in that final line: the principle of otherness, opposition, difference itself is the point, not necessarily the qualities which comprise each side of the opposition. The vehemence with which he polices these differences must also be seen as a prime symptom that they are breaking down. But what I want to focus on here is how Lawrence figures this principle of sexual 'otherness' as key to 'the magic and the dynamism' of the sexual act. It is an opposition which is vigilantly policed, and which mutates at key moments in Lawrence's work into a conflict of domination, in scenes when power relations become explicit. When that otherness is breached, when the gap is stopped, sexuality is perverted. Since Lawrence sets such store by the sexual act as font of all human and social health, it is clearly important to look at its role in his work, as well as to look at the contradictions that these representations pose for his understanding of what writing can and cannot do.

In this chapter I will look specifically at the central Lawrentian experience of sexual fulfilment, partly because it is so crucial to his philosophy and narratives, and partly because since the 1960 trial the popular image of Lawrence has been that of writer of 'dirty books'. I will, however, also explore the darker pleasures of Lawrentian sex by first framing discussion with a brief account of how saturated his whole corpus is with images of sexual power, fleshing out those scenarios of dominance, victimization, sado-masochistic pleasure and submission I discussed earlier. Inequality is Lawrence's celebrated norm; sexual battles precede sexual consummation. Since sex itself is so crucial to Lawrence, I will then look at some scenes of what we might call 'bad' sex, sex done wrong, sex which (for Lawrence, anyway) damages. I will also think about how race infuses Lawrence's sexual agenda, by looking at the human sacrifice scene with which 'The Woman Who Rode Away' (1924) culminates, as a scene of perverse sexuality which dare not speak its name. This, indeed, is sometimes literally true, for at key moments of crisis Lawrentian sex slips into silence.

FRUSTRATION AND FULFILMENT: *THE TRESPASSER* AND *LADY CHATTERLEY'S LOVER*

Written very early in Lawrence's career, well before his protracted battles with the moral majority of his day over explicitness in print, the short novel *The Trespasser* is a tale of sexual evasion. In many ways it prefigures the obsessions of his last novel *Lady Chatterley's Lover*, except that what remains unfulfilled and thwarted in the early text is consummated in the later one. If there are crisis moments in *The Trespasser*, they take place between paragraphs and in ellipsis. Compare this novel, only Lawrence's second, to his final work: the differences in sexual representation which mark these two moments at the beginning and the end neatly embody Lawrence's changing attitude to censorship. When in *The Trespasser* it is the kiss which manifests desire, in *Lady Chatterley's Lover* sex itself becomes the site of prime human experience.

The Trespasser is the story of an affair between Helena, a fanciful but inhibited young woman, and her married lover Siegmund. The two go on holiday to the Isle of Wight, and their differing attitudes to sexual desire sit uneasily between them, until Siegmund, maddened by unfulfilment, kills himself. Though a much slighter tale than the later novels which deal with these issues more fully, it does clearly set up some central Lawrentian concerns. The constraint early twentieth century (family) life brings to bear on desire, but more importantly the way that the individual internalizes that constraint and acts as both generator and check to his own desire, is crucial. Once again the split subject and the sexually frustrated subject seem more interesting than their wholesome and fulfilled counterparts. Despite the intense passion which magnetizes Siegmund and Helena, they never entirely drop their guard, and what happens between them is shrouded in evasion – here Lawrence shrinks from explicitness. The ghostly estrangement which we looked at in chapter 2, characterizing Siegmund's visits to his family home, infuses much of the book: reserve, detachment and alienation are its keynotes, although this is contrasted with the immediacy of the lush English arcadia Lawrence evokes in the Isle of Wight sequence.

But Siegmund and Helena's is as much a mis-meeting as a meeting, a relationship of mutually fulfilled narcissism. Helena is 'like the sea' ('It spends its passions upon itself', (*T.* 76)), not centrally interested in the confrontation with otherness which Lawrentian sex ideally brings about. Her key moments with Siegmund are the satisfaction of a self-focused rather than an other-focused desire:

> That night she met his passion with love. It was not his passion she wanted, actually. But she desired that he should want *her* madly, and that he should have all – everything. (*T.* 87)

Siegmund too experiences his delight in Helena more through the way in which his passion for her mediates his feelings about his own body. Indeed, the bodily manifestation of Siegmund's desire is detailed with a luscious sympathy which is close to homoerotic, most manifest in Lawrence's careful account of the man's sexual fantisizing. Perhaps the most sensual moments in the book take place not when the lovers embrace, but when Siegmund, alone, revels in thoughts of his own body as well as of Helena's. Meanwhile Helena is to him literally a closed book, a different language of being, 'written in characters unintelligible to him and to everybody' (*T.* 155).

The heightened sensual moments of the Isle of Wight section notwithstanding, what the novel really explores is the aftermath of this climactic time, when Siegmund and Helena go their separate ways. As a whole it moves from desperation through overwrought desire to disappointment, thwarted fulfilment and then despair and tragedy. Helena and Siegmund's is a 'poetic stimulation' (*T.* 179) not a physical one – certainly not a mutually driven sexual stimulation. Helena partly prefigures Miriam's final fear or repulsion of the body in *Sons and Lovers*: in the freshness of daylight Helena tries 'to clear away the soiling of the last night's passion' (*T.* 76). Siegmund goes back to the home which is not a home, wanting what he cannot have, and split by conflicting desires:

> I cannot live alone. I shall want Helena – I shall remember the children. If I have the one, I shall be damned by the thought of the other. This bruise on my mind will never get better. (*T.* 162)

Part of Lawrence's agenda in *The Trespasser* is to explore the psychological damage inflicted by thwarted desire. Part of his agenda in *Lady Chatterley's Lover* is to show that fulfilled desire can fundamentally transform the subject and her world. If early in his writing Lawrence tried to write the subject differently, dispensing with 'the old stable ego of the character', his last works are marked by a serious attempt to rewrite the literary body. Connie Chatterley is married to a man whose body is violently 'rearranged' by World War I (he is shipped back from Flanders 'more or less in bits'). Although 'the bits seemed to grow together again', Clifford is left, master of the family line, the stately home, and the mining business, but paralysed from the hips down. There is a sense that the sexlessness which is now actualized in body is only the external metaphor for the sexlessness which had always prevailed between the Chatterleys. Connie is bereft, but when she meets the estate gamekeeper, Mellors, and begins an affair with him, her body is rejuvenated. The illicit lovers develop their connection until Connie becomes pregnant, Clifford is told, and divorce proceedings begin (this was, remember, written at a time when divorce was rare – Frieda's split from her first husband was famously scandalous). The novel ends with the *promise* of a happy ending:

Connie is alone, but the lovers plan to live together. This is another open-ended ending, but *Lady Chatterley's Lover* strives for certainty on one crucial issue: the bodily certainty which Connie and Mellors's sex has established.

Sex between Connie and Mellors is the heart of *Lady Chatterley's Lover*, just as sex itself is at the heart of Lawrence's writings. It is another of Lawrence's late apocalyptic tales, or rather post-apocalyptic tales. 'The cataclysm has happened, we are among the ruins', runs the second sentence of the novel: 'We've got to live, no matter how many skies have fallen'. This is another exploration and affirmation of 'life': Connie's body 'connect[s Mellors] up again' (*LCL* 118), so much so that after their first sexual encounter he half regrets that he has been brought back, as if from the dead: '"It's life," he said. "There's no keeping clear. And if you do keep clear, you might almost as well die"'. 'Life' re-emerges full blooded in this English pastoral story of a woman's salvation through sex.

But what kind of sex? The novel has also been read as Lawrence's consummate statement on phallic sexuality, although readers have found it less misogynistically overbearing than earlier 'phallic' writings, largely because of its privileging of Conne's point of view. Connie is actively sexual: her simple statement in justification of her desire – 'I liked your body' – was a rare and shocking statement of active female sexuality. After experiencing simultaneous orgasm with Mellors, she begins to realize 'the depth of the other thing in her':

> Another self was alive in her, burning molten and soft and sensitive in her womb and bowels. And with this self, she adored him, she adored him till her knees were weak as she walked. (*LCL* 135)

In their last major sexual encounter in the book Connie experiences a 'phallic hunting out' which finally renders her shameless:

> In this short summer night she learnt so much. She would have thought a woman would have died of shame. Instead of which, the shame died. Shame, which is fear: the deep organic shame, the old, old physical fear which crouches in the bodily roots of us, and can only be chased away by the sensual fire, at last it was roused up and routed by the phallic hunt of the man, and she came to the very heart of the jungle of herself. (*LCL* 247)

Sex accesses the beast in the self's jungle. Instead of conscious shame and moral response, Connie finds openness and accesses what Lawrence calls in *Studies of Classic American Literature* her IT.

Not only, then, might sexuality change your life, it should change the whole economy of yourself, of your body, too. The resurrected post-apocalyptic body which Connie accesses can tell truths more directly than any form of conscious or linguistic discourse – Mellors's penis has 'got his root in my soul' (*LCL* 211). Lawrence's body language is always honest: his bodies, when allowed to speak, cannot lie. In fact sex is the *only* possibility of truth-telling in Lawrence, a truth we must listen to or perish. 'You don't mistrust with your body, when your blood comes up', Connie says to Mellors. 'Let your mind mistrust. What does it matter!' (*LCL* 204–5)

That sex takes us further, changing the body and its knowledges, is also at issue in *Sons and Lovers*. Sex slides subjects into a pantheistic reverie, so that even Paul and Clara are unrecognizable to themselves:

> When he came to, he wondered what was near his eyes, curving and strong with life in the dark, and what voice it was speaking. Then he realised it was the grass, and the peewit was calling. The warmth was Clara's breathing heaving. He lifted his head and looked into her eyes. They were dark and shining and strange, life wild at the source staring into his life, stranger to him, yet meeting him. (*SL* 398)

In a similar post-coital episode in *The Rainbow*, sex between Ursula and Skrebensky staged in the darkness at the edge of the town is represented as impersonal, outside of history and social connection:

> When she rose, she felt strangely free, strong. She was not ashamed – why should she be? He was walking beside her, the man who had been with her. She had taken him, they had been together. Whither they had gone, she did not know. But it was as if she had received another nature. She belonged to the eternal, changeless place into which they had leapt together. (*R*. 451)

Although connections are suggested between their bodies and the corpulence of the natural world around them (they are under an oak tree, the wind is blowing), this experience is given to be both bodily *and* transcendent. Lawrence's 'darkness' enables this self-overcoming *through* the body, through, too, the body of another. This is 'natural', but it also re-writes, reconceives, what 'natural' is: 'it was as if she had received another nature', Lawrence writes. So we would be wrong to think of Lawrence simply as celebrator of a banal form of romantic nature-worship. Here the natural is open to dynamic re-inscription in the melting-pot of human experience. It is not that Ursula and Skrebensky, or Connie and Mellors, have left culture and escaped into nature, but that their connection has rewritten the natural.

But this dark new nature is also the agent of division. I have said that Ursula is part of Lawrence's ongoing project to reconceive the literary ego as multiple and divided. When she then returns to her family it is as a double-self:

> Her soul was sure and indifferent of the opinion of the world of artificial light. ... she felt herself belonging to another world ... Her everyday self was just the same. She merely had another, stronger self that knew the darkness. (*R.* 451–2)

Similarly, the new sexual self which Connie discovers is contradictory: she has been stirred alive into a state which is not straightforward: 'again she was divided between two feelings', Lawrence writes after the pair have had something of a tiff; 'resentment against [Mellors], and a desire to make it up with him' (*LCL* 170). Her new double-self performs a kind of organic unifying process on her, reuniting the post-apocalyptic fragments, but separating her into two selves, one of which learns from the other, or submits to the other. Connie is 'tormented by her own double consciousness' (*LCL* 172). Indeed, this uneasiness characterizes the whole of the couple's relationship, at least when they are not actually making love. Lawrence wants us to read this tension differently: not as the sign of failure but as the context within which a new kind of relationship can be forged.

It is also a new way of conceiving conflict. Mellors and Connie's verbal struggles are not battles for domination, but the context of self-overcoming. Even the phallic worship of the 'Power Period' novels is toned down. Instead, phallic love becomes Lawrence's name for something conjured up in the contract between man and woman. Connie addresses Mellors's penis as a separate being (the 'John Thomas' of the alternative version of this novel, *John Thomas and Lady Jane*). Looking at the flaccid organ, she says,

> And now he's tiny, and soft like a little bud of life! ... And he comes so far into me! You must never insult him, you know. He's mine too. He's not only yours. He's mine! And so lovely and innocent! (*LCL* 210)

I am reminded of that moment of supreme gender-bending in Angela Carter's *The Passion of New Eve*, when Tristessa the transvestite's penis becomes the ultimate sign of his/her femininity: 'his instrument of mediation between himself and the other'.[1] Connie's claim on it for her pleasure, and for theirs as a pair, suggests that the organ acts in a way which is not entirely body-specific, which makes it as much a part of the woman's sexual anatomy as the man's. Phallic sexuality in this novel is then something which passes across and between male and female desire.

Of course, Lawrence's penises appear in an exclusive heterosexist context, and the book as a whole is guilty of this. At one point Mellors lurches into an appalling tirade against his ex-wife, whose actively controlling sexuality he diagnoses as lesbianism: 'When I'm with a woman who's really Lesbian, I fairly howl in my soul, wanting to kill her' (*LCL* 203). (The rather nasty *Pansies* poem 'Ego-Bound Women' (*Poems*, 475) echoes this sentiment). Elsewhere in Lawrence, same-sex desire is rather more openly explored – Birkin and Gerald wrestling on the carpet in *Women in Love* is one clear example, as is the sexual relationship which develops between the teenage Ursula and her female teacher in *The Rainbow* (although this is undercut by Ursula's subsequent guilty repulsion and regret). The primacy of heterosexuality in Lawrence might be the literalization of that dictum of opposition with which I started: 'the magic and the dynamism rests on *otherness*'. Clearly he cannot conceive of 'otherness' existing within and between the same sex – there is something about the mix of male and female which produces sparks, and which needs the conjunction of men's and women's bodies.

What, then, was so shocking about this novel that it could not be published legally in Britain until 1960? Even seventy years after it was written, it still seems quite explicitly rendered, making liberal use of common sexual words. Thirty years after

Lawrence's death, Penguin Books finally published the complete novel, and their subsequent trial under the 1959 Obscene Publications Act became the test case defining what the Act covered. The argument that sexual explicitness could be mitigated by artistic merit, and that words in themselves did not necessarily constitute a 'depraving or corrupting' force, not only changed the world of publishing in Britain, but repeated many of the terms of self-defence Lawrence had set out in his two important essays written in justification of the then-unpublishable novel itself, 'Pornography and Obscenity' and '*A Propos* of *Lady Chatterley's Lover*'. Clearly, too, there is a peculiarly British anxiety about class being worked through here, both in the novel itself and in British responses to class during the middle of this century. The prosecution at the trial wondered if potential readers would want their servants to read it: clearly any novel which described so explicitly the pleasures of a cross-class union and which positioned the woman as more socially powerful was bound to be deemed dangerous. But the implications were also both that the working class (from which the writer of the novel came) should be protected by the law, and that the 'we' who were to decide on the novel's obscenity were the sort who would keep servants. The jury balked on both counts, and the acquittal of Penguin signalled the start of a very different set of relationships between state and reader.

Connie and Mellors's love is actually quite romantically conceived (*Lady Chatterley*'s working-title was 'Tenderness'), and the novel has serious philosophical pretensions. The notion that sex can save is endearingly, and naïvely, represented. As Mellors and Connie's relationship develops, their existence focuses more on what happens between their bodies in Mellors's sparse, bare little cottage, and less on the socially conscious outer world. Intensely embodied their relationship may be, as Lawrence strives to affirm the materiality of love. But it is also sternly non-materialistic, an island or escape into bodily commitment. That Mellors and Connie are true to each other is a hallmark of the tale, and its legal defence. Rather than advocating promiscuity, the novel conceives itself as an experiment in one-to-one committed sexual romance. This is Lawrence as (to borrow Frieda's phrase), 'the last word in Puritanism'. That sex can be liberating and self-transforming (a reading which was particularly favoured after the trial in the 1960s) is argued both through the sex itself, and in moments such as the famous scene when Connie threads flowers through Mellors's pubic hair as the pair discuss the ills of money, advanced industrial consciousness and modern relationships. Then they run outside and dance naked in the rain. Does this mean that this is what we should do – that the novel as 'depraving and corrupting' would potentially encourage us to do the same? Lawrence's case for his work in his two pornography essays is quite specific. It is not that he would change our acts but our thoughts. 'I want men and women to be able to *think* sex, fully, complete, honestly, and cleanly', he writes in '*A Propos* of *Lady Chatterley's Lover*'. 'Even if we can't *act* sexually to our complete satisfaction, let us at least think sexually, complete and clean' (*P2* 489–90). For the body to be free the mind must be too: 'The mind has an old, grovelling fear of the body and the body's potencies. It is the mind we have to liberate, to civilise on these points' (*P2* 491). But this is strangely rendered through a language of evasion. In particular, at moments of 'phallic hunting out' something slips off the page in order to be entirely authentic. Sexual passion gives way to something rather more mystical, and mystified. Sex is a channel, a doorway into something else. It takes recognizable literary characters who we have known as 'Constance Chatterley', 'Rupert Birkin' or 'Ursula Brangwen' and changes them. What the self is when subject to the natural, and what the body is when it undergoes the alchemy of authentic sex, remains unclear.

GOOD SEX AND BAD: PERVERSION, FREUD AND *THE PLUMED SERPENT*

So if what is 'natural' is not clear, what is 'unnatural' is positively obscure. Contrast the above descriptions of Mellors and Connie's consummation with this infamous scene from *The Plumed Serpent*, which also recalls Freud's favouring of the 'mature' vaginal orgasm over the 'phallic' clitoral one:

> She realized, almost with wonder, the death in her of the Aphrodite of the foam: the seething, frictional, ecstatic Aphrodite. By a swift instinct, Cipriano drew away from this in her. When, in their love, it

> came back on her, the seething electric female ecstasy, which knows such spasms of delirium, he recoiled from her....
>
> ...By a dark and powerful instinct he drew away from her as soon as this desire rose again in her, for the white ecstasy of frictional satisfaction, the throes of Aphrodite of the foam. She could see that to him, it was repulsive.
>
> And she, as she lay, would realize the worthlessness of this foam-effervescence, its strange externality to her. It seemed to come upon her from without, not from within. And succeeding the first moment of disappointment, when this sort of 'satisfaction' was denied her, came the knowledge that she did not really want it, that it was really nauseous to her. (*PS* 439)

Something has shifted. This is pleasure, it is satisfaction, but it is somehow the wrong sort. And not only is pleasure turned into unpleasure here by virtue of the fact that the woman takes control, she is also finally made – despite her frustration – to engage in her own diagnosis of disappointed desire. You want it but you don't, it was exciting but it wasn't really, a thrill which is finally bad for you (or bad for *him*, and what's bad for him is bad for you). In *Sexual Politics* Kate Millett argues that all Lawrence is interested in is denying woman pleasure: 'Ladies', writes Millett, 'don't move. In both [*The Plumed Serpent* and *Lady Chatterley*] there are a number of severe reprimands delivered against subversive female "friction"'.[2] But this passage from *The Plumed Serpent* is probably nearer to Freud than to the 'lie back and think of England' school of female sexual propriety. In the section on 'Leading Zones in Men and Women' in the *Three Essays on the Theory of Sexuality*, Freud discusses how women must 'put aside their childish masculinity'[3] of clitoral pleasure and adopt a more adult and advanced emphasis on the vagina. For Lawrence, too, there is good sex and bad sex; against the 'Aphrodite of the foam' type is posited an alternative image of good sex, 'beyond knowing', a 'mindless communion of the blood':

> And [Cipriano], in his dark, hot silence would bring her back to the new, soft, heavy, hot flow, when she was like a fountain gushing noiseless and with urgent softness from the volcanic deeps. Then she was open to him soft and hot, yet gushing with a noiseless soft power. And there was no such thing as conscious 'satisfaction'.

Let us linger in the world of 'bad' sex for a moment. By bad sex I mean not unsatisfying sex, but sex deemed wrong, unnatural, distorted, perverse. The 'nauseous' aspect of Kate's foamy frenzy, a satisfaction which comes from without not from within, situates this pleasure directly in the world of the perverse. For the *Oxford English Dictionary*, perversity is law-breaking. The pervert is

> Turned away from what is right... Obstinate and persistent in what is wrong... Disposed to be obstinate or contrary to what is true or good or to go counter to what is reasonable or required.

Perversion here is directly linked to transgression: the true and the good and the law are established, and perversion counters each of these, turning away from them, challenging them. Perversion is then defined entirely with reference to the law. It has no truth of its own except that given to it by its other. Strangely, however, Freud starts his *Three Essays* not with an account or normality, but with a long discussion of aberration. The rule of normality – the true and the good – is absolutely *not* set up before the way in which it is broken is described. In these essays at least, *perversity precedes normality.*

When Freud goes on to define 'normality', however, his account is extraordinarily strict. The 'normal sexual aim is regarded as being the union of the genitals in the act known as copulation', he writes, but even within this normality what he calls 'perversion' exists – foreplay, looking, touching the sexual object before arriving at it, even kissing (these all being deferrals of the moment of 'union of the genitals'). Each of these serve to put off the moment of union. They act as a detour on the way to copulation, and they extend the pleasure beyond the scope of intercourse through exploration of other areas of the body. Perversions, he writes,

> are sexual activities which either (a) extend, in an anatomical sense, beyond the regions of the body that are designed to sexual union, or (b) linger over the intermediate relations to the sexual object which should normally be traversed rapidly on the path towards the final sexual aim.[4]

Perversion, then, is sex in the wrong place, at the wrong time, or focusing on the wrong part of the body. It is anticipation with no arrival, it is non-genital, it is the controlled taking over the role of controller. Let us remember this as we look now at

Hermione in *Women in Love*, and at the fateful but nameless 'Woman Who Rode Away'.

In her important discussion of 'Masochism and Male Subjectivity', Kaja Silverman notes that the *Oxford English Dictionary* definition of the perverse still elaborates its terms with etymological reference to a statement of Francis Bacon, which gives these examples of generalized perversity:

> women to govern men...slaves freemen...being total violations and perversions of the laws of nature and nations.

The perverse is then the world turned upside-down – it is women precisely *not* 'yielding precedence to a man'. In this spirit, the protracted diatribe against the 'cocksure' woman which takes place across Lawrence's career might be deemed a Bacon-ite statement on the 'violation of the laws of nature': when women wear the trousers, the whole world turns perverse. As I explored in relation to *The Fox* earlier, one key component of Lawrence's misogyny is his figuring of women in terms of light, vision, visual sex, a pornographic sadistic gaze. For Lawrence the gaze is not male (as it is for many feminist cultural theorists since the 1970s), but female, and the object of the gaze, of the woman's heterosexual look, is the dark male body. Masculinity as spectacle is thus writ large in Lawrence's corpus. Not only does Lawrence, in those words of Norman Mailer 'illuminate the passion to be masculine', he illuminates our, and our heroine's view of the male body, so that it becomes the most visibly alluring object in his work. Women, for Lawrence, are the prime seers of Western culture, and since the weight of his philosophy favours the darkness of consummate sex, the visual, the cinematic, and consequently the feminine are denigrated and marginalized. They are perverse.

HERMIONE'S MIRRORS

Women in Love's Hermione is an important blueprint for the visually conscious woman who emerges in a number of Lawrence's texts, established as such through Birkin's earlier character assassination which focuses on her pornographic sex. I now want briefly to return to Hermione, as a figure of egoistic knowing *will*, certainly, but as one who expresses this will through a perverse sexuality. For Hermione is both Eve (fixated on mental knowledge) and the Lady of Shalott (only able to respond to the world through the mirror):

> You've got that mirror, your own fixed will, your immortal understanding, your own tight conscious world, and there is nothing beyond it. There, in the mirror, you must have everything. (*WL* 91)

Hermione's problem here is, according to Birkin, her 'bullying will. You want to clutch things and have them in your power... [b]ecause you haven't got any real body, any dark sensual body of life....You have only your will and your conceit of consciousness, and your lust for power, to know' (*WL* 92). Sensuality and darkness thus lie on the one (masculine) side; will, consciousness, knowledge and above all vision lie on the other (feminine) side.

As one of Bacon's women who governs man, Hermione is then 'obstinate and persistent in what is wrong' *for women* in Lawrence. If 'proper' Lawrentian sexual release comes through Dark sex, Hermione's comes through voluptuous (illuminated, and visual) violence. More interesting than *what* she is doing, is *what* what she is doing *does to her*:

> Terrible shocks ran over her body, like shocks of electricity, as if many volts of electricity suddenly struck her down...A terrible voluptuous thrill ran down her arms – she was going to know her voluptuous consummation. Her arms quivered and were strong, immeasurably and irresistibly strong. What delight, what delight in strength, what delirium of pleasure! She was going to have her consummation of voluptuous ecstasy at last! It was coming! In utmost terror and agony, she knew it was upon her now, in extremity of bliss....Her heart was a pure flame in her breast, she was purely unconscious in ecstasy. (*WL* 162–3)

What is *wrong* with this – what makes it bad sex? This clearly *is* sex, as is evidenced by the way in which Lawrence figures Hermione's sexual response – the lapses of consciousness are there, the terror and bliss, the unconscious ecstasy, the promise of climax, the thrill. The terms which conflate egoistic annihilation in the moment of consummation for Hermione (her mind is 'blotted out'), with ascendancy to a greater sense of self for Birkin and Ursula, are uncannily similar. Yet it's a sexual response to a strictly non-sexual act: this is an act of violence, as she is about to hit Birkin with a lapis lazuli paper-weight. So what is the difference between this response and Ursula's to Birkin later in the book (which I'll say more about later)? And what is the difference between this act of violence, from a woman to a man, and the central act of violence in 'The Woman Who Rode Away', from a man to a woman?

One answer to the first set of questions has to come from how this relates to the whole image of Hermione which emerges through the book. On the one hand, this is a perverse pleasure precisely because it happens before the arrival does – it 'linger[s] over the intermediate relations'. This is foreplay which *becomes the act itself*, an orgasmic response not to the moment of completion but to the stages which lead towards that moment. Hermione's sex is then not so much misdirected as charged by hesitation: she spends the whole of this section getting off on the *anticipation*, rather than 'properly' enjoying the arrival: 'she *was going to* know...to have'; 'It *was coming*'. But what kind of 'coming' *is* this? The point is surely that she *hasn't* come, only that she thinks she *will*. Anticipation is as good as it gets: almost as if to punish her, Lawrence ensures that coming is exactly what will *never come* for Hermione: 'Her fingers were in the way and deadened the blow'; 'it was not somehow complete' – this is a sexual disappointment akin to Cipriano's denial of Kate's 'Aphrodite' pleasure. Women who want the wrong thing are thus guaranteed never to get it. Whether it is clitoral orgasm (a frictional white ecstasy) or Hermione's 'electric' pleasure in violence, the goal is the wrong one. As we saw in chapter 3, it is not that Lawrence finally advocates peace and harmony in a relationship of non-violence. It is that this female sadism, and Kate's clitoral desire, are resolutely non-phallically orientated.

Thus we can read the sexuality of the moment at which this 'bullying' finally gets its way (when Hermione lashes out at Birkin) through a larger picture of her visual and conscious perversity. One sense in which this represents the 'wrong' sex rather than the 'right' is in its conflation of the terms of illumination with the terms of perverse pleasure. Electricity is one of the key forces of modernism, one of the physical components of the 'shock of the new', and here it is Hermione's element – an alternative form of Kate's sexual friction, but also the power which 'lights up' her perverse, sado-masochistic consciousness. She is 'charged', she is 'shocked'; the electric passion and the exquisite pain she feels connect to make her literally illuminated:

> it was one convulsion of pure bliss for her, *lit up* by the crushed pain of her fingers. (*WL* 163)

What is disturbing about this is the way in which it directly and deliciously aligns the element of vision – light – with a tormented sexual drive the text can only condemn. Illumination plus pain (hers and Birkin's) equals a perverse bliss which finds its pleasure on the wrong side of the tracks. Mellors's rapture in Connie's body is an attempt to rewrite beauty as a non-visual sexual-aesthetic, a 'live, warm beauty of contact, so much deeper than the beauty of vision' (*LCL* 125). For Hermione, the visual is the medium through which the body receives all its sensual signals. Vision is the director of all physical power.

This then is sex, but it's the wrong sort. Indeed, by the writing of the Chatterley novels the idea of bad sex taking place across culture, and good sex saved for the precious moments of intimate isolation between the lovers, has become fully developed. So when Mellors discusses the 'bad' sex which has taken place between himself and his first wife Bertha, this is only the crystallization of what's going on everywhere across their diseased culture. Indeed, the closer you read late Lawrence, the harder it becomes to separate inauthentic sex which takes place in bed, and inauthentic acts which characterize the culture as a whole. Cipriano might save Kate, but it's too late for Bertha:

> Gradually I got sick of it: and she got worse. She sort of got harder and harder to bring off, and she'd sort of tear at me down there, as if she was a beak tearing at me. By God, you think a woman's soft down there, like a fig. But I tell you the old rampers have beaks between their legs, and they tear at you with it till you're sick. Self! Self! Self! all self! tearing and shouting! They talk about men's selfishness, but I doubt if it can ever touch a woman's blind beakishness, once she's gone that way. Like an old trull! (*LCL* 202)

Unpleasant as this passage is, it confirms a strain in Lawrence's thought which runs across his work. Rather than seeing the relationship as a contract, Bertha sees Mellors as an object, the medium for her pleasure. Of course, this is partly what Connie has done, in liking Mellors's body and claiming his penis as her own. But Lawrence argues for sex as exchange not objectification – Mellors says 'I could never get my pleasure and satisfaction of *her* unless she got hers of me at the same time' (*LCL* 206). Like the 'Aphrodite of the foam' passage, sex for Bertha is entirely focused on her clitoral 'beak', the instrument through which woman governs man and which renders her politically as well as sexually 'perverted'. If there is a puritanism in all this, it's in Lawrence's denial that being a sex object can be positive, and his insistence that wholesome spiritual exchange via the body is the only way to proceed.

But some perversions are clearly more perverse than others. As Kaja Silverman writes of Freud – and this is equally true of Lawrence – 'what is acceptable for the female subject is pathologised for the male',[5] and vice versa. Here what is acceptable for the male is pathological – perverse – in the female, but the point of this is that Bertha's warped and aggressive sexuality is only part of the bigger, sicker, picture. Bad sex is implicated in – and perhaps it causes – a whole range of societal ills. This can be argued through various strands – industrial control of landscapes and bodies, male impotence in bedroom and boardroom, the centrality and (for Lawrence) over-importance of the visual in culture, identity and sex, or – in my conclusion – words and silence.

ANTICIPATION AND RACE: 'THE WOMAN WHO RODE AWAY'

Lawrence has a keen sense of colour. We might address this by plotting out an elaborate symbolic system which could be mapped onto his wider philosophical and ideological framework; or we might turn to his painting. But 'colour' also certainly means race for Lawrence, especially in the post-war American and Mexican writings. Light and Darkness is an all-pervasive opposition here, which is always mapped onto sexual judgement and value. But black and white, especially in the texts Lawrence wrote after his first arrival in America, also means Indian and Anglo-European. These texts, particularly *The Plumed Serpent*, 'The Woman Who Rode Away', and the collection of travel essays *Mornings in Mexico*, argue for a strong relationship between the subject and the 'spirit of place' of landscape and culture, which Lawrence saw as most authentically lived by the Indian civilizations of southwest America and Mexico.

'Darkness' and 'light' thus also need to be understood as a specifically racial opposition: preferring the 'dark' of unconscious consummation (mostly identified as masculine) over the 'light' of mental reason and control (feminine) also means – in the American texts, at least – choosing black over white, Orient over Occident, Indian over Westerner. During a brief period in the early-to-mid-1920s Lawrence thus takes his Dark/Light philosophical and sexual opposition to its logical racial conclusion. In his second essay on Fenimore Cooper, Lawrence had advocated a form of hybridity, a kind of racial openness, which would efface difference but which also acknowledges that difference can only be overcome if 'white consciousness' changes:

> The white man's spirit can never become as the red man's spirit. It doesn't want to. But it can cease to be the opposite and the negative of the red man's spirit. It can open out a new great area of consciousness, in which there is room for the red spirit too. (*SCAL* 57)

However, in both *The Plumed Serpent* and 'The Woman Who Rode Away', it is whiteness which must 'yield precedence', and black power which is in the ascendant: 'The power of the world . . . was now fading in the blue eyes, and dawning in the black', he writes in one of Kate Leslie's meditations towards the end of *The Plumed Serpent*:

> The power of the world was dying in the blond men, their bravery and their supremacy was leaving them, going into the eyes of the dark men, who were rousing at last. (*PS* 415)

However, this potentially laudable prophecy of a racial redistribution of power inevitably becomes unpalatably sexually weighted when black is read as male, and white as female. Kate is the sign of the West here, Ramón and Cipriano the 'rousing' embodiments of future black control. Initially established as independent and economically active, Kate is the site upon which the move from dominator to dominated is staged. She is set up only to be knocked down, empowered only so that she can subsequently occupy the position of defeated or submissive whiteness. A sexual contract, in which (white) woman is eventually figured as debtor and (dark) man as creditor, is filtered through a discourse of racial difference and the justification of anti-imperialistic rebellion. We might even say that Lawrence uses a racial discourse only in order to make his sexual discourse stick. She is white, he is Indian: Kate 'owes' the Mexicans something both as symbol of imperialist oppression and as a woman who has foolishly gone above herself. The Mexican revolution thus becomes individualized as Ramón and Cipriano's subsumption of Kate.

Something of the same story is told more starkly and emblematically in 'The Woman Who Rode Away'. The woman's unnatural whiteness is detailed with grotesque relish, a whiteness which strips her of sexuality, making her 'some giant, female white ant' (*WRA* 57). This is not a clean whiteness; indeed, dispatching her seems to be itself an act of cleansing (the black eyes of her executioners have 'a terrible glittering purity', *WRA* 60). Crucially, her execution is the supreme moment of pay-off in a sexual-racial contract wrought far more crudely than that of *The Plumed Serpent*, the moment which allows the 'mastery that man must hold' to '[pass] from race to race' (*WRA* 81), from white back to black. The white woman's death allows the Indian to 'be full of power, like a spring day. But the white people will be a hard winter, without snow'[6] (*WRA* 75). Thus Lawrence might be seen to be working with a fairly conventional racial/coloured system, through which he threads a sexual set of judgements, and within which he argues for darkness and against whiteness.

I want to build on this with an analysis of 'The Woman Who Rode Away' which sees it as perverse *and* as a consummate image of ideal desire in Lawrence. How do race and perversity connect in this story? As the case of Hermione has shown, perversion isn't only about straying from the norm. It is also about lingering on, and enjoying too much, moments through which one should 'properly' pass. In Freud's definition, if the goal is suspended for too long, the process becomes its other: remember that perversity resides in '*linger[ing]* over the *intermediate* relations to the sexual object which should normally be traversed *rapidly* on the path towards the final sexual aim'.

There is then a link (which again Kaja Silverman makes) between that key psychoanalytic concept of deferred action and perversity. This is usually understood as a term concerned with memory, involving an idea or image being planted in the mind at one moment of development, and then reactivated at a later stage – the comprehension of the original moment being 'deferred' until that later stage. As Freud wrote, 'Memory is present not once but several times over'.[7] For Silverman it is also about anticipating the moment of arrival precisely in order to put it off for as long as possible. Enjoying the 'foreplay' of suspense, extending the wait for as long as you can, this is perverse.

We might say that 'The Woman Who Rode Away' is an exercise in this activity. Clearly it must be read as an elaborate fantasy, but what kind of fantasy is it? The white heroine, descendant in a line of Lawrentian 'cocksure' women who know too much and submit too little, shakes off her headstrong heritage and plunges into nothingness. She rides away to an inevitable fate which sees her murdered – or sacrificed – at the hands of the men of an obscure tribe of Indians she latches onto after leaving her old life. She gets on her horse, rides into the mountains, and becomes a sacrificial victim – that's basically it. But did she fall or was she pushed? What desires animate the process of her killing? Hers is a movement towards masochistic self-abnegation and sacrifice which ends at the point of a knife: even before she is dead, she is dead. The whole story is articulated from the point of view of one who feels herself already written out of the script of her own life. When still alone, and 'feeling like a woman who has died and passed beyond', the woman

> was not sure that she had not heard, during the night, a great crash at the centre of herself, which was the crash of her own death. (*WRA* 51)

It is that double negative ('she was *not* sure that she had *not* heard') which articulates the absent-presence of the woman's existence. When the Indians appear, she 'feel[s] more as if she had died', as they look at her 'with a black, bright inhuman look, and saw no woman in her at all. As if she were some strange unaccountable *thing*' (*WRA* 54). Yet, soon after, she experiences a 'thrill of exultation'. She knew she was dead' (*WRA* 55). This is repeated a number of times, as if it's not enough to make the woman die once. She must experience her death through a series of 'thrilling' pre-emptive shocks, and if we take the death itself as a supreme articulation of sado-masochistic penetration writ large, these moments constitute a kind of fatal foreplay. 'A long, long night, icy and eternal, and she was aware that she had died' (*WRA* 56); 'She listened as if from the dead' (*WRA* 64); 'she seemed at last to feel her own death, her own obliteration' (*WRA* 69). And it is not only that she dies before she is dead; these precursive 'little deaths' also strip her of her sexuality:

> They could not see her as a woman at all. As if she were not woman. As if, perhaps, her whiteness took away all her womanhood. (*WRA* 57)

So how is this one of Lawrence's sexual fables? 'The Woman Who Rode Away' can and must be read as a key articulation of precisely two opposing perverse desires. Either it is an exercise in the sadism of the one who spins the fantasy (not the woman, but her writer). Or it is an exultant indulgence in life after death before death, a feminine masochism which desires to have the self put down at every turn, so that eventually that self disappears. Either way, the story is an exercise in perversity. *Falling* or plunging into her own exquisite nothingness, the woman desires a radical self-abnegation. If, however, we read this as a story animated by the desire to kill, by a movement which *pushes* the woman to her doom, it becomes a key articulation of male as well as writerly sadism, which strings out the build-up to the final knifing for as long as possible – an exercise, then, in sadistic suspense.

Kate Millett famously read the story as symbolic 'in the same sense as a head exposed on London Bridge'. This is, again as Simone de Beauvoir put it, one of Lawrence's blueprints for women. But according to Nietzsche and to Michel Foucault after him, heads on London Bridge also served a different function. They not only reinforced the audience's sense of the moral code which needed to be followed to the letter, but offered a limited outlet for a range of sadistic desires which could be vented through this bloody voyeurism. In the violent cultural history which Nietzsche posited, an appetite for blood needed to be satisfied, and the public execution was one arena in which this took place. If this is true also of texts, what does a story like 'The Woman Who Rode Away' offer to its audience?

And whose point of view does this story take anyway? If it is the woman's, what is so sexy about imagining you're dead – what identifactory pleasures are at stake when woman is put to the stake? Perhaps this is the 'little death' reversed: if orgasm is like death, maybe identifying with the dead, or the doomed, is also sexual. In her reading of *The Plumed Serpent*, Millett writes that 'The novel's point of view is the woman's; its point of interest is the two attractive males'.[8] She then goes on to call Kate 'a female impersonator', meaning that any femininity which is unappealing must really be masculinity in drag (Angela Carter took a hilarious position on this in 'Lorenzo as Closet Queen'[9]). For Millet femininity is used as a vehicle through which Lawrence can explore both his own feminine passivity and his homosexual desire for Cipriano:

> [Kate's] vertiginous passivity is not only an admonition to her sex, but something the author appears to enjoy playing at himself. Through the device of the heroine, Lawrence has found a vehicle to fantasize what seems to be his own surrender to the dark and imperious male in Cipriano.[10]

Whilst generally designating Lawrence's tales as forms of sex-crime in which the author-perpetrator is clearly positioned, Millett is also here willing to discuss the possibility that who is doing what to whom, and how this affects narrative and readerly identification, is complicated. If the narrative voice speaks from the woman's side, this effectively feminizes the reader into identification with her position, regardless of the reader's own gender outside of the text. In entering into identification through the text, the reader is de-sexed, or otherwise-sexed. Through identification, he or she becomes in part the penetrated thing – not primarily the hand that wields the knife, but also the sacrificial body.

As the story progresses, so the woman slips into a masochistic delirium of self-abnegation, leading only to the point of her sacrifice. Yet a simultaneous process of de-sexualization takes place, paradoxically as the gaze of the Indians becomes more central:

> She was the more puzzled, as there was nothing sensual or sexual in the look. It had a terrible glittering purity that was beyond her. She was afraid, she would have been paralysed with fear, had not something died within her. (*WRA 60*)

Not only does the woman feel herself dead, she feels death beginning to touch her; 'The Woman Who Rode Away' becomes the story of fatal foreplay:

> The white-haired, glassy-dark old man moistened his finger-tips at his mouth, and most delicately touched her on the breasts and on the body, then on the back. And she winced strangely each time, as the finger-tips drew along her skin, as if Death itself were touching her. (*WRA* 63)

We are still in the realm of sexual anticipation. If arrival is the guarantor of sexual health, this is a story which fails to arrive, which delays too much. The story's climax is dripping with the language of sexual penetration – the imagery is hardly subtle. But this is finally a case of *coitus interruptus*, since the knife never actually *arrives in* body of its victim. Perhaps then the most tormenting thing about 'The Woman Who Rode Away' is not anything actually done to bodies, but its denial of a final complete moment of closure in sexualized death. The final two sentences of the penultimate paragraph are still anticipatory:

> In absolute motionlessness he watched till the red sun *should* send his ray through the column of ice. The old man *would* strike, and strike home, accomplish the sacrifice and achieve power. (*WRA* 81, my italics)

Suddenly the shift of identification moves from the woman to her executioner, but crucially *his* moment of arrival slips beyond the final full stop. If the best has yet to come, it never comes. Finally, this emerges as the most perverse story of all: a protracted exercise in erotic suspense, which makes us make do with the pleasures of apprehension rather than those of release. The rest is silence.

Conclusion: Sex words and silence

our activity has lost its meaning
we are ghosts, we are seed;
for our word is dead
and we know not how to live wordless.

– 'Dies Irae', from *Pansies* (*Poems*, 510)

I conclude with lots of questions. Although Lawrence has long been known as a sexually explicit writer, forms of sexual experience exist at the margins of his writing which cut against the grain of how authentic sexuality is identified in his work overall, and which constitute Lawrence's guilty pleasures. Here 'perversity' is not a simple term. An indulgence in transgression, or experiences properly associated with the opposite sex, figure powerfully in many texts, but not simply as objects of Lawrence's wholesome critique. Sexually speaking, Lawrence can be (and is) in (at least) two different places at once – inviting identification with his masochistic, sacrificial figures of dissolute femininity and with his authentic dark males. He also wants both speech and silence, writing what should not be written, all at the same time.

'What happened' to Kate in *The Plumed Serpent* 'was dark and untellable' (*PS* 439) – 'dark and untellable', and yet Lawrence tries to tell us it. Good sex is not just frictionless and vaginal, but crucially purified of language. So how is one to represent this – what happens to 'untellable' sex when you try to tell on it? Mellors feels 'the cruel sense of unfinished aloneness, that needed a *silent* woman folded in his arms' (*LCL* 144, my emphasis). Yet Connie is anything *but* silent, in that her narrated point of view, articulating to the last exquisite physical detail the twists of her awakening sex, dominates the text. Whilst one voice urges us not to kiss and tell, still another must speak the unspeakable.

In all this perversion, prevarication and power-play, what Lawrentian pleasure actually is becomes more and more obscure. Is it sensory plenitude or momentary annihilation? Mutual exchange or phallic domination? These questions themselves beg a series of more specific questions about the relationship between writing and sex in Lawrence, or what written sex might be. Can there be, for Lawrence, an 'authentically' sexual way of bringing sex into language? Do words already have their own sexuality? Can sex exist *without* words – can it *really* be seen (even in Lawrence) as extra- or pre-linguistic, an act beyond discourse? These are questions at the heart of his project – they are also questions, I think, at the heart of pornography, although Lawrence hated the word being applied to his work.

However, this whole issue – indeed the whole chequered history of *Lady Chatterley's Lover* – revolves around a paradox. Sex is rightly silent for Lawrence, just as it is authentically 'dark', slipping off the page throughout his writing. It happens between paragraphs – as with that moment in the grass between Paul Morel and Clara, which only emerges after it has happened, with 'When he came to'. It happens in the midst of breathtaking evasion, it is allowed to slip away behind a limited lexicon of orgasmic gestures. Here is an example from the famous scene on the hearth-rug in the 'Excurse' chapter of *Women in Love,* and here I am not particularly interested in how the lovers get to this point (or the fact that this sexual experience is primarily anal), but in what happens to Lawrence's subjects at the moment of *jouissance*:

> She seemed to faint beneath, and he seemed to faint... It was a perfect passing away for both of them, and at the same time the most intolerable accession into being, the marvellous fullness of immediate gratification, overwhelming, outflooding from the source of the deepest life-force, the darkest, deepest, strangest life-source of the human-body, at the back and base of the loins. After a lapse of stillness, after the rivers of strange dark fluid richness had passed over her, flooding, carrying away her mind and flooding down her spine and down her knees, past her feet, a strange flood, sweeping away everything and leaving her an essential new being, she was left quite free, she was free in complete ease, her complete self. (*WL* 396)

The key elements of sex figured as the little death are here, which (again) aligns Lawrence's view of orgasmic *jouissance* with Freud's, despite the disagreements of Lawrence's psychoanalysis books. In *Beyond the Pleasure Principle* Freud writes that

> We have all experienced how the greatest pleasure attainable by us, that of the sexual act, is associated with a momentary extinction of a highly intensified excitation.[1]

This for Freud is linked to 'the most universal endeavour of all living substance – namely to return to the quiescence of the inorganic world'.[2] So, contrary to Lawrence's position, the extinction of the conscious self in Freud's articulation of 'the little death' is not a *reconnection* with the Life Principles, but an early, untimely echo of the moment at which we will cease to be *even alive* – an experience not just 'beyond the pleasure principle', but beyond the organic.

What then is Lawrence striving to 'go beyond' in all this overwhelming passing away, fainting, flooding, darkness and deepness? Is this about *absence*, about a moment of exquisite relief in not-being, a sacrifice of the ego which gives the self a momentary blissful experience beyond itself, beyond its own agency? Is this an example of what Freud called primary masochism, that desire for non-being which aims for total annihilation of self and will? If this is so, how do we bring these 'passing away' phrases together with the experience of possession – *self*-possession – which punctuates the passage? – 'at the same time the most intolerable *accession into being*, the marvellous *fulness* of immediate *gratification*' which left her 'an *essential new being*...quite free...in complete ease, *her complete self*' (my emphasis). What is being lost and what is being gained? *Is* this pleasure, or is it – like Freud's death-drive – *beyond* the pleasure principle? Or is it somehow both – pleasure *and* beyond pleasure, self and non-self, utterance and silencing?

One response might come through thinking about this in directly 'New French Feminist' terms, as Sandra Gilbert does in her 1986 introduction to Hélène Cixous and Catherine Clément's *Newly Born Woman*, where she likens feminine *jouissance* of French theory, emerging primarily from the work of psychoanalyst Jacques Lacan, to the ecstasy of Lawrence's sexualized female subjects:

> Didn't D. H. Lawrence – in *Lady Chatterley's Lover* and elsewhere –

> begin to outline something oddly comparable to Cixous's creed of woman before she did? Describing the cosmic mystery of Connie's *jouissance*, this often misogynistic English novelist defines an 'orgasm' whose implications, paradoxically enough, appear to anticipate the fusion of the erotic, the mystical, and the political that sometimes seems to characterise Cixous's thought on this subject, for Connie's coming to sexuality is also a coming to selfhood and coming away from the historically hegemonic Western 'nerve-brain' consciousness that would subordinate body to mind, blood to brain, passion to reason.[3]

So *Jouissance* is by this account a kind of politicized ecstasy; it is a moment of overcoming which also overthrows egoistic and institutional forms of control. As Gilbert puts it in her definition, the word has '*simultaneously* sexual, political, and economic overtones. Total access, total participation, as well as total ecstasy are implied'.[4] But for Lawrence, as for Lacan, 'enjoyment' is not a primary – or desirable – part of the whole experience. Indeed, Lacan suggests that translating *jouissance* as 'enjoyment' might be inadequate, when he is faced with the Madison Avenue billboard commandment 'Enjoy Coca-Cola'. For Lawrence too, enjoyment is not only not enough, but may be too much – as passive consumption, or misdirected pleasure, better to have no 'enjoyment' at all.

I am not interested in thinking about what image of sexual connection is being represented, but rather about how the possibility of that representation connects with wider things Lawrence has to say about sex and language. At moments like those between Birkin and Ursula or Connie and Mellors, Lawrence starts a fierce battle between language and textual sex which he cannot hope to resolve. The questions I am asking of the late stories are all part of a bigger question I am asking of Lawrence's corpus as a whole: how can he write about sex when – according to the agenda he has set himself – sex should not be written about? What happens when he does? Does this explain his unfinishedness – the consummation which can only fall off the edge of the text?

Sex which speaks, which is visible, which is 'light', bears the brunt of all of Lawrence's negative terms. There are examples of this right across Lawrence's work and we have seen many of them: the fight for 'correct' sex against the incorrect form which prevails in modern culture is already bubbling up in his earliest texts, and is developed through to the posthumously published work. If 'good sex' is partly about passing away into nothingness but also, at the same time, about ascending to a fuller sense of self in *Women in Love*, the alternatives are ironically about conscious linguistic focus and *naming* your pleasure.

The question of silence is a key focus, since what Lawrence finds himself saying about the Word is central to what he says about sex. It is also centrally paradoxical. In a sense, Lawrence continues to develop the position he sketches out through Anna in *The Rainbow*:

> But the *language* meant nothing to her: it seemed false. She hated to hear things expressed, put into words. (*R.* 106)

In *Lady Chatterley's Lover*, words act on subjects rakishly, sadistically, gaining a seductive control which must be resisted:

> How she hated words, always coming between her and life: they did the ravishing, if anything did: ready-made words and phrases, sucking all the life-sap out of living things.

Words, then, *ravish* the soul; their relationship to life is orally sadistic, they vampirically suck out the blood. Connie here is the resistant prey of language, relating to the word as the victim relates to her sadist (as Mellors relates to Bertha). Again Lawrence's sexual thinking echoes Freud's. For Lawrence, like Freud, we are immersed in the world of sex even in our connection with language. But *unlike* Freud, for Lawrence words act on the lives – indeed the 'life' – of subjects as sadists act on the bodies of their sexual objects. In *The Plumed Serpent*, Kate rallies against

> the ugly blows of direct, brutal speech! She had suffered so much from them. Now she wanted this veiled elusiveness in herself, she wanted to be addressed in the third person.

Again words – here in the form of speech – are capable of personal assault. They brutalize the authentically silent, wordless self: they violate. Once Kate has conceived of 'submission absolute', she becomes 'wordless':

> Language had abandoned her, and she leaned silent and helpless in the vast, unspoken twilight of the Pan world. . . .

> Her world could end in many ways, and this was one of them. Back to the twilight of the ancient Pan world, where the soul of woman was dumb, to be forever unspoken. (*PS* 325–6)

If Kate's silencing is connected to her increased ability to respond authentically in sex (her 'veiled elusiveness' is part of her cleaving to Cipriano), then the crime of speech is directly bound up with sex gone wrong. I am reminded of a French Feminist position, that of Luce Irigaray's advocacy in *This Sex Which is Not One* of 'getting rid of words in order not to become fixed, congealed in them'.[5] But how can any writer advocate *in writing* getting rid of words?

This is not the only paradox at work here. If the sex of the dark hero should not be spoken, what is Mellors doing in speaking Bertha's? Perhaps, we might say, her version of sex is already so corrupted that the extra 'ravishment', the 'ugly blows' of words, do not matter. Perhaps part of the problem is that this is sex which *must* be spoken, and this too constitutes part of the 'tearing' which Mellors experiences. Nevertheless there is an uneasy voyeurism about his representation which highlights the nefarious, bitchy pleasure the speaker takes in *showing* us his verbal prey. If language curtails the free play of the essentially pre-linguistic, silent dark self, how can this sexual play be written? This is where Lawrence's championing, on the one hand, of the novel as 'the one bright book of life', and his philosophical preference for silence and darkness, on the other, must come into conflict across his texts. If perversity is 'turn[ing] away from what is right', being 'obstinate and persistent in what is wrong', then is this also what is happening in Lawrence in the very act of writing sex? Perhaps the evasions of that passage from *Women in Love* are enforced by the fact that at this moment in cultural history sex is being conceived as an act which moves the subject to the brink of death, passes her over it, and then allows her to return (in Bataille's famous view in *Literature and Evil* of Emily Brontë's vision: 'Eroticism is the approval of life up until death'). Perhaps these evasions are also bound up with the knot into which Lawrence has tied himself. Decreeing the essential truth of a sex which is silent, pre-linguistic, he then tries to speak and write that sex.

I have constantly returned to the question of unfinishedness in this analysis: Lawrence's resistance to the closed text, the dynamic of anticipation and non-arrival which marks his narratives and undermines their apparently definitive polemic, his maddening ability to say and then to unsay something in the same breath. He writes in his 1919 'Foreword to *Women in Love*',

> Any man of real individuality tries to know and to understand what is happening, even in himself, as he goes along. This struggle for verbal consciousness should not be left out in art. It is a very great part of life. It is not superimposition of a theory. *It is the passionate struggle into conscious being.*[6]

Perhaps 'struggle' is unfinishedness, it is the contradictory self of 'Death is not Evil, Evil is Mechanical', it is the dynamic of saying and not saying a thing at the same time.

Lawrence gives the last word of his last novel to writing itself. In a bizarre but rather endearing epistolary speech made by Mellors's 'John Thomas' at the end of *Lady Chatterley's Lover*, the letter carries the voice of sex to its reader. Here those two most crucial elements, writing and sex, are linked in a way which bypasses everything else, but which still echoes with the tones of absence and unfinishness:

> 'Now I can't even leave off writing to you.
>
> 'But a great deal of us is together, and we can but abide by it, and steer our courses to meet soon. John Thomas says goodnight to Lady Jane, a little droopingly, but with a hopeful heart –' (*LCL* 302)

There is not even a final full stop.

Notes

INTRODUCTION: LIFE WORKS

1. Jane Davis, 'Envoi: the genie in the second-hand bookshop', in *Rethinking Lawrence*, edited by Keith Brown (Milton Keynes: Open University Press, 1990), pp. 182 and 181 respectively.
2. F. R. Leavis, *D. H. Lawrence: Novelist* (London: Chatto and Windus, 1967), 9.
3. Leavis, 11.
4. Leavis, 15.
5. Alison Light, 'Feminism and the Literary Critic', in *LTP*, no. 2 (1983), 64.
6. Carol Dix, *D. H. Lawrence and Women* (London: Macmillan, 1980), p. ix.
7. Dix, 24.
8. Sheila MacLeod, *Lawrence's Men and Women* (London: Grafton Books, 1987), 7.
9. Pinkney writes 'To write an Eliotic, English-realist novel in the first decade of this century... was an impossible project, leading in its very break-up to important theoretical discoveries about the nature of such realism itself'. Tony Pinkney, *D. H. Lawrence* (Hemel Hempstead: Harvester Wheatsheaf, 1990), 12.
10. From Lawrence's 'Foreword to *Women in Love*', which is collected in the Cambridge edition of the novel, edited by David Farmer, Lindeth Vasey and John Worthen (Cambridge University Press, 1989), 485.

CHAPTER 1. PHILOSOPHIES

1. Sigmund Freud, 'The Ego and the Id' (1923), in *On Metapsychology*, Pelican Freud, vol. 11 (Harmondsworth: Penguin, 1984), 362.
2. Paul Delaney, *D. H. Lawrence's Nightmare* (Brighton: Harvester Press, 1979), 18.

CHAPTER 2. FAMILY ROMANCES

1. Sheila MacLeod, *Lawrence's Men and Women*, 8.

CHAPTER 3. GENDER AND ITS DIFFERENCES

1. Alastair Niven, *D. H. Lawrence: The Novels* (Cambridge: Cambridge University Press, 1978), 169.
2. Keith Brown, 'Introduction', *Rethinking Lawrence* (Milton Keynes: Open University Press, 1990), p. xiv.
3. Hilary Simpson, *D. H. Lawrence and Feminism* (London: Croom Helm, 1982), 88.
4. C. H. Rolph, *The Trial of Lady Chatterley: Regina v. Penguin Books Limited* (Harmondsworth: Penguin, 1961), 8.
5. Carol Dix, *D. H. Lawrence and Women* (London: Macmillan, 1980), p. x.
6. Norman Mailer, *The Prisoner of Sex* (London: Weidenfeld & Nicolson, 1971), 152.
7. Sheila MacLeod, *Lawrence's Men and Women*, 10.
8. See Linda R. Williams, 'The Trial of D. H. Lawrence', in *Critical Survey*, vol. 4, no. 2, 1992.
9. Norman Mailer, *The Prisoner of Sex*, 109.
10. Kate Millett, *Sexual Politics* (London: Virago, 1982), 265.
11. Norman Mailer, *The Prisoner of Sex*, 134.
12. Mailer, 151–2.

CHAPTER 4. DANGEROUS PLEASURES AND DARK SEX

1. Angela Carter, *The Passion of New Eve* (London: Virago, 1982), 128.
2. Kate Millett, *Sexual Politics*, 240.
3. Freud, *Three Essays*, 144.
4. Freud, *Three Essays*, 61–2.
5. Kaja Silverman, *Male Subjectivity at the Margins* (New York and London: Routledge, 1992).
6. This is the essence of the story, although it is also infused with a curious colour-coded mythology. The Indian village has a wintry whiteness, but the Indians themselves are 'all brown and yellow and black hair, and white teeth and red blood.' The woman is only white and blue, 'the colour of the wind... the colour of the dead' (*WRA* 74).
7. Sigmund Freud, *The Complete Letters of Sigmund Freud to Wilhelm*

Fliess 1887–1904 (Cambridge and London: Harvard University Press, 1985), 207. For a fuller discussion of deferred action and memory see chapter 4, 'Too Early and Too Late: Mrs Oliphant and the Wolf Man', in my introduction to psychoanalytic literary theory, *Critical Desire: Psychoanalysis and the Literary Subject* (London: Edward Arnold, 1995).

8. Kate Millett, *Sexual Politics*, 283.
9. Angela Carter, 'Lorenzo as Closet Queen', in *Nothing Sacred* (London: Virago, 1982).
10. Kate Millett, *Sexual Politics*, 284.

CONCLUSION: SEX WORDS AND SILENCE

1. Sigmund Freud, *Beyond the Pleasure Principle*, in *On Metapsychology*, Pelican Freud, vol. 11 (Harmondsworth: Penguin, 1984), 336–7.
2. Freud, ibid., 336.
3. Sandra Gilbert, Introduction to Hélène Cixous and Catherine Clément, *The Newly Born Woman* (Manchester: Manchester University Press, 1986), p. xvii.
4. Gilbert, ibid, 165.
5. Luce, Irigaray, 'This Sex Which is Not One', in *This Sex Which is Not One* trans. Catherine Porter with Carolyn Burke (Ithaca and New York: Cornell University Press, 1985), 29.
6. D. H. Lawrence, 'Foreword to *Women in Love*', ibid., 486.

Select Bibliography

WORKS BY D. H. LAWRENCE

The Penguin editions of Lawrence's works have long been the most accessible editions in print. However, the exhaustive and definitive Cambridge University Press editions which are gradually appearing are now increasingly available in paperback, and should be consulted if possible. For reasons of widespread availability I have referred to Penguin texts in this study.

Apocalypse (Harmondsworth: Penguin, 1979).

Aaron's Rod (Harmondsworth: Penguin, 1977).

The Complete Poems of D. H. Lawrence, ed. Vivian de Sola Pinto and Warren Roberts (Harmondsworth: Penguin, 1977).

The Complete Short Novels (Harmondsworth: Penguin English Library, 1982).

England, My England (Harmondsworth: Penguin, 1979).

'The Escaped Cock', in *The Complete Short Novels* (Harmondsworth: Penguin English Library, 1982).

Fantasia of the Unconscious and Psychoanalysis and the Unconscious (Harmondsworth: Penguin, 1974).

The First Lady Chatterley (Harmondsworth: Penguin, 1978).

The Fox, in *The Complete Short Novels* (Harmondsworth: Penguin English Library, 1982).

John Thomas and Lady Jane (Harmondsworth: Penguin, 1977).

Kangaroo (Harmondsworth: Penguin, 1972).

Lady Chatterley's Lover (Harmondsworth: Penguin, 1994).

The Lost Girl (Harmondsworth: Penguin, 1977).

Love Among the Haystacks and Other Stories (Harmondsworth: Penguin, 1978).

Mornings in Mexico/Etruscan Places (Harmondsworth: Penguin, 1977).

The Mortal Coil and Other Stories (Harmondsworth: Penguin, 1977).

Mr Noon (Cambridge: Cambridge University Press, 1984).

Phoenix: The Posthumous Papers of D. H. Lawrence, ed. Edward D. McDonald (London: Heinemann, 1936).

Phoenix II: Uncollected, Unpublished and Other Prose Works by D. H. Lawrence, ed. Warren Roberts and Harry T. Moore (London: Heinemann, 1968).

The Plumed Serpent (Harmondsworth: Penguin, 1977).

The Princess and Other Stories (Harmondsworth: Penguin, 1980).

The Rainbow (Harmondsworth: Penguin, 1979).

Sea and Sardinia (Harmondsworth: Penguin, 1979).

Selected Essays (Harmondsworth: Penguin, 1978).

Sons and Lovers (Harmondsworth: Penguin, 1994).

St Mawr, in *The Complete Short Novels* (Harmondsworth: Penguin English Library, 1982).

Studies in Classic American Literature (Harmondsworth: Penguin, 1977).

Three Plays (*A Collier's Friday Night / The Daughter-in-Law / The Widowing of Mrs Holroyd*) (Harmondsworth: Penguin, 1985).

The Trespasser (Harmondsworth: Penguin, 1994).

Twilight in Italy (Harmondsworth: Penguin, 1977).

The White Peacock (Harmondsworth: Penguin, 1979).

The Woman Who Rode Away and Other Stories (Harmondsworth: Penguin, 1978).

Women in Love (Harmondsworth: Penguin, 1989).

The seven-volume Cambridge University Press complete edition of Lawrence's letters is definitive. A good abridged collection is *The Selected Letters of D. H. Lawrence*, edited by James T. Boulton (Cambridge University Press, 1997). See also the three-volume collection of *Letters*, edited by Boulton *et al.* in 1979, also published by Cambridge.

BIOGRAPHICAL AND CRITICAL STUDIES

Armin, Arnold, *D. H. Lawrence and America* (London: Linden Press, 1958).

——— *D. H. Lawrence and German Literature* (Montreal: Heinemann, 1963).

Beauvoir, Simōne de, 'D. H. Lawrence or Phallic Pride', in *The Second Sex* (Harmondsworth: Penguin, 1981).

Bloom, Harold (ed.) *D. H. Lawrence's Women in Love*, Modern Critical Interpretations (New York: Chelsea House, 1988).

Brown, Keith (ed.), *Rethinking Lawrence* (Milton Keynes: Open University Press, 1990).

Burgess, Anthony, *Flame into Being: The Life and Work of D. H. Lawrence* (London: Heinemann, 1985).

Carter, Angela, 'Lorenzo as Closet Queen', in *Nothing Sacred* (London: Virago, 1986).

Chambers, Jessie ('E. T.'), *D. H Lawrence: A Personal Record* (Cambridge: Cambridge University Press, 1980).

Clarke, Colin (ed.), *The Rainbow and Women in Love*, Casebook series (Basingstoke: Macmillan, 1969).

—— *River of Dissolution: D. H. Lawrence and English Romanticism* (London, 1969).

Corke, Helen, *D. H. Lawrence: The Croydon Years* (Austin, Texas: University of Texas Press, 1965).

Delaney, Paul, *D. H. Lawrence's Nightmare: The Writer and his Circle in the Years of the Great War* (Brighton: Harvester Press, 1979).

Delavenay, Emile, 'D. H. Lawrence and Sacher-Masoch', in the *D. H. Lawrence Review*, vol. 6, Summer 1973.

Dix, Carol, *D. H. Lawrence and Women* (London: Macmillan, 1980).

Feinstein, Elaine, *Lawrence's Women: The Intimate Life of D. H. Lawrence* (London: HarperCollins, 1993).

Fernihough, Anne, *D. H. Lawrence: Aesthetics and Ideology* (Oxford: Clarendon Press, 1993).

Ford, George H., *Double Measure: A Study of the Novels and Stories of D. H. Lawrence* (New York: Holt, Rinehart and Winston, 1965).

Gordon, David J., *D. H. Lawrence as a Literary Critic* (New Haven and London: Yale University Press, 1966).

—— 'Sex and Language in D. H. Lawrence', in *Twentieth Century Literature: A Scholarly and Critical Journal*, 27, 4, Winter 1981.

Heywood, Christopher (ed.), *D. H. Lawrence: New Studies* (London: Macmillan, 1987).

Holderness, Graham, *D. H. Lawrence: History, Ideology and Fiction* (Dublin, 1982).

Hough, Graham, *The Dark Sun: A Study of D. H. Lawrence* (Harmondsworth: Penguin, 1961).

Kalnins, Mara (ed.), *D. H. Lawrence: Centenary Essays* (Bristol: Classical Press, 1985).

Kermode, Frank, *Lawrence* (London: Fontana, 1973).

Lawrence, Frieda, *Not I, But the Wind...* (London: Granada, 1983).

Leavis, F. R., *D. H. Lawrence: Novelist* (London: Chatto & Windus, 1967).

—— *Thought, Words, Creativity: Art and Thought in Lawrence* (London: Chatto & Windus, 1979).

Light, Alison, 'Feminism and the Literary Critic', in *Literature Teaching Politics*, no. 2, 1983.

Luhan, Mabel Dodge, *Lorenzo in Taos* (London: Martin Secker, 1933).

MacLeod, Sheila, *Lawrence's Men and Women* (London: Heinemann, 1985).

Maddox, Brenda, *D. H. Lawrence: The Story of a Marriage* (New York:

Simon & Schuster, 1994).

Mailer, Norman, *The Prisoner of Sex* (London: Weidenfeld and Nicolson, 1971).

Meyers, Jeffrey (ed.), *D. H. Lawrence and Tradition* (London: Athlone Press, 1985).

—— *The Legacy of D. H. Lawrence: New Essays* (London: Macmillan, 1987).

Miko, Stephen J. (ed.), *Twentieth Century Interpretations of 'Women in Love'* (New York: Prentice Hall, 1969).

Millett, Kate, 'D. H. Lawrence', in *Sexual Politics* (London: Virago, 1981).

Moore, Harry T., *The Priest of Love: A Life of D. H. Lawrence* (Harmondsworth: Penguin, 1976).

Nin, Anaïs, *D. H. Lawrence: An Unprofessional Study* (London: Neville Spearman, 1961).

Niven, Alastair, *D. H. Lawrence: The Novels* (Cambridge: Cambridge University Press, 1978).

Nixon, Cornelia, *Lawrence's Leadership Politics and the Turn against Women* (Berkeley: University of California Press, 1986).

Pinkney, Tony, *D. H. Lawrence* (Hemel Hempstead: Harvester Wheatsheaf, 1990).

Poole, Roger, 'Psychoanalytic Theory: *St Mawr*', in *Literary Theory at Work: Three Texts*, ed. Douglas Tallack (London: Batsford, 1987).

Rolph, C. H., (pseudonym of C. R. Hewitt), *The Trial of Lady Chatterley: Regina V. Penguin Books Limited* (Harmondsworth: Penguin, 1961).

Sagar, Keith, *D. H. Lawrence: Life into Art* (Athens, Georgia: University of Georgia Press, 1985).

Salgãdo, Gãmini, 'D. H. Lawrence as a Literary Critic', in *London Magazine*, vol. 7, February 1960.

—— 'Taking a Nail for a Walk: on reading *Women in Love*', in *The Modern English Novel: The Reader, the Writer and the Work*, ed. Gabriel Josipovici (London: Open Books, 1976).

Salgãdo, Gãmini, and G. K. Das (eds), *The Spirit of D. H. Lawrence*, Centenary Studies (London: Macmillan, 1988).

Sanders, Scott: *D. H. Lawrence: The World of the Major Novels* (New York: Viking, 1974).

Scheckner, Peter, *Class, Politics and the Individual: A Study of the Major Works of D. H. Lawrence* (Rutherford, New Jersey: Fairleigh Dickinson University Press, 1985).

Simpson, Hilary, *D. H. Lawrence and Feminism* (London and Canberra: Croom Helm, 1982).

Smith, Anne (ed.), *Lawrence and Women* (London: Vision Press, 1978).

Spender, Stephen (ed.), *D. H. Lawrence: Novelist, Poet, Prophet* (London: Weidenfeld and Nicolson, 1973).

Veitch, Douglas W., *Lawrence, Green and Lowry: The Fictional Landscape of*

Mexico (Waterloo, Ontario: Wilfred Laurier University Press, 1978).
Widdowson, Peter (ed.), *D. H. Lawrence*, Longman Critical Readers series (London and New York: Longman, 1992).
Williams, Linda Ruth, *Sex in the Head: Visions of Femininity and Film in D. H. Lawrence* (Hemel Hempstead: Harvester Wheatsheaf, 1993).
——— 'The Trial of D. H. Lawrence', in *Critical Survey*, vol. 4, no. 2, 1992.
Williams, Raymond, *The English Novel: From Dickens to Lawrence* (London, 1971).
Wilt, Judith, *Ghosts of the Gothic: Austen, Eliot and Lawrence* (Princeton, New Jersey: Princeton University Press, 1980).
Worthen, John, *D. H. Lawrence and the Idea of the Novel* (London: Macmillan, 1979).

OTHER WORKS REFERRED TO IN THE TEXT

Carter, Angela, *The Passion of New Eve* (London: Virago, 1982).
Freud, Sigmund, *Beyond the Pleasure Principle*, in *On Metapsychology*, Pelican Freud, vol. 11 (Harmondsworth: Penguin, 1984).
——— *The Complete Letters of Sigmund Freud to Wilhelm Fliess 1887–1904* (Cambridge and London: Harvard University Press, 1985).
——— 'The Ego and the Id' (1923), in *On Metapyschology*, Pelican Freud, vol. 11 (Harmondsworth: Penguin, 1984).
——— *Three Essays on the Theory of Sexuality*, in *On Sexuality*, Pelican Freud, vol. 7 (Harmondsworth: Penguin, 1977).
Gilbert, Sandra, Introduction to Hélène Cixous and Catherine Clément, *The Newly Born Woman* (Manchester: Manchester University Press, 1986).
Irigaray, Luce, 'This Sex Which is Not One', in *The Sex Which is Not One*, trans. Catherine Porter with Carolyn Burke (Ithaca and New York: Cornell University Press, 1985).
Silverman, Kaja, *Male Subjectivity at the Margins* (New York and London: Routledge, 1992).
Williams, Linda Ruth, *Critical Desire: Psychoanalysis and the Literary Subject* (London: Edward Arnold, 1995).

Index